Brad Willis
2011

BLUESTOCKING

Bud Willis

authorHOUSE®

AuthorHouse™
1663 Liberty Drive, Suite 200
Bloomington, IN 47403
www.authorhouse.com
Phone: 1-800-839-8640

First published by AuthorHouse 9/21/2009

ISBN: 978-1-4490-2742-1 (e)
ISBN: 978-1-4490-2741-4 (sc)

Printed in the United States of America
Bloomington, Indiana
This book is printed on acid-free paper.

Margaret Louise Dryden age 22

Emma Mae Dryden with Granddaughters Ann and Martha 1944

Comments from readers of
pre-published Bluestocking...

"Reading your book was sheer pleasure and enjoyment. I laughed out loud...funny and full of surprises."

Terry Geremski
Catawba Island, Ohio

"One minute I was laughing out loud and the next minute I was crying."

Sherry Sorrells
Lewisburg, TN

"You have a work of art that has the potential of going beyond the reason it was written."

David Waggener
Columbia, KY

"I thoroughly enjoyed this book. I thought of so many things while reading it and getting to that pinpoint of light. Your stories would spark a memory and I would take it from there. A very enjoyable and well written book!

Jerry Simon
Indianapolis, IN

"I wouldn't change a thing. I finished it at two in the morning."

Blanche McClure
Tullahoma, TN

"Once I began reading it I couldn't seem to stop. Thank you for bringing back so many of my childhood memories. I both laughed and cried. A bowl of pinto beans and chopped onions is still one of my favorite meals."

Sandy Hartley
Port St. Lucie, FL

Comments from NBC Today
Show segment...

"It was truly refreshing to have the story to talk about last night with friends and relatives instead of watching the current news."

Judy Brown
Memphis, TN

"Thank you for the honor of performing for you and the country... (on the Today Show)...a morning I will never forget."

Aaron Lazar
New York, NY

"What an extraordinary piece really...and Bud told the story so beautifully."

Leslie Dagenbach
Maineville, Ohio

"Of all the people I have met, including rock stars and politicians and the like, its people like you who stand out as examples of who I would like to be."

Hank Bonecutter
Clarksville, TN

"Absolutely outstanding! Semper Fi!

Roger Henry
Manassas, VA

"What a wonderful story...we are still wiping tears from our eyes."

Reece and Ruby Manyweathers
Kent, England, UK

"I am sitting here trying to type this message with tears running down my cheeks."

Mike Curtin
Naples, FL

"This is one amazing and inspiring story and I was able to hear it directly from you. It was awesome."

Neil Fleming
Landsdale, PA

Who Is I

When I learned to write in college, we were supposed to make an outline and stick to it. You may remember doing that. In today's world, the great writers write "in the dark." They get into a quiet room alone, and let their imagination take them wherever it wants to go. After several hours of this, they have written what they call "inventory." After days of that kind of discovery, a story starts to emerge. Characters come in and out of the story from nowhere, and they sometimes say things the writer is unable to understand until it is revealed to him several pages later. This is creative writing today. *"Don't let your story get in the way of your writing,"* is a comment I heard at a writer's conference. I can't wait to write like that, but this book is a memoir and is supposed to be true. I don't have the luxury of that kind of creative chaos. But the reader should be forewarned that any story becomes fiction as soon as the writer puts the word "I" into it. Also, memoir means memory, and memories are like an old car that's been stored in a barn for a long time; you might get it cranked up, but it would be foolish to take it on a long road trip.

The first part of my road-trip memoir is called exposition. This is where I get to give as much background as necessary to set the stories up, so they will be more meaningful. I went a little overboard on this because there was some genealogy that I wanted to include. After several revisions and rewrites, I decided to put most of that background information in a separate section in the back of the book, which I called historical outtakes. It's easy to get bogged down in somebody else's genealogy and lose interest in the rest of the story. But it still may be the most important part of the story. Everyone needs to know where they came from. Otherwise, how will you ever know who you really are? The apple doesn't fall far from the tree, you know.

You may find a few mistakes in spelling or grammar if you look carefully. I blame computers for that, and those maniacally addictive emails and "crackberry" text messages. Our culture has gotten lazy in the way we write. However, the good news is, there's more communication than ever because of technology. It's fast and easy, and it's not *all* bad. Anyway, I hope you will forgive my typing or mental errors. Part of the charm of life is that we are all human, and make mistakes.

I was invited to appear on the TODAY show while I was writing this book. My wife, Lee, seemed to think that there was one particular story that was important enough for the whole world to hear, so I went along with her. I decided to include that TV experience in the book because of the enormous public reaction to the show. If you hang in there throughout that story, you will be well rewarded.

In the early stages of writing this book I paid for a consultation with a memoir specialist named Michael Steinberg. I sent him 30 pages of my manuscript, and later sat with him for an hour to hear his advice. For the first half hour, he rambled on about a book he was writing called *"Extra Innings,"* without mentioning my book. Finally, I pointed to the pages that I had mailed him. I could see that he had scribbled some notes on them, and I asked him what he meant by the first note, "Who is I?"

He explained that I had begun writing in the first person, without bothering to explain who "I" is, in the current sense. In other words, the "I" in the stories is a different person from the "I" that is writing the stories. The writer has added about 60 years, put on a few extra pounds, and hopefully gained a little more wisdom over time.

So, it's a two "I'd" book. Then, Mike asked me what the book was about. I had already told him in a one-page synopsis that it was stories from my childhood, growing up in a small town, and how my mother had a tough road raising nine kids by herself with no income. We both had to stifle a yawn after that. Mike said a book should be about a single thing, as small as a pinpoint of light, and every word in the book should lead the reader to that light. *"Writing is a craft,"* he said.

I want to be a crafty writer and I will listen to any advice I can get. But my first book is not intended to be an important book. I'm not shooting for the Pulitzer here. The purpose of this book is to entertain people who can relate to these stories, especially the people who helped to make them. This is a "friends-and-family" book. But, I want the reader to be pulled into the stories and be able to "feel" them, as well as being moved by the message on the way to that pinpoint of light.

A single pinpoint of light! What a great concept! Every writer needs to drive his stories to a single destination to keep the reader pressing forward. I can assure you that there is a single point of light in this book, and I will take you there. But along the way, you will be reminded of your own childhood, and your own family. You will laugh out loud several times. And, there will be times when you may want to have a small box of tissues handy.

Thank you for buying my book, but more importantly, thanks for reading it.

Bud Willis

Contents

PROLOGUE

New York City

November 11, 2008, 12:30 pm

It was Veterans Day, and traffic had been brutal coming into Manhattan from JFK that morning. It took an hour and a half. President Bush was in town, and some of the streets were blocked off for the annual Veterans Day parade. The driver had to let us off three blocks from our hotel. The hotel desk clerk advised us that our room would not be ready until 3 pm, so I had to get dressed in the locker room of the men's spa at the Club Quarters Hotel. We had been "surprised" the day before by an on-the-air phone call from Kathie Lee Gifford. My wife and I had taken a 6 am flight from Naples, Florida. Suddenly, I was part of the drama of day time television, appearing on a show that a few weeks ago I didn't even know existed. Things were getting off to a shaky start, and beads of sweat were starting to form on top of my bald head. So far, I wasn't getting treated like a TV celebrity.

I met Jayme Baron in front of Dean and Deluca across from the NBC News building at 12:30 pm. Jayme was the associate producer of the TODAY show. She had invited me and my wife, Lee, to New York to film a story I had written for one of their programs. Back in September, Lee was running on the treadmill and watching TV, while I was working on this very book you are reading. When she finished her workout, she walked out, wringing wet, and breathlessly announced that I needed to write a story for a contest that she had just heard about on TV. It was for a show called "Everyone Has a Story." I told her emphatically, that there was absolutely no way that would ever happen. *"Not in a million years!"* Anyway, here I am in

New York with my story. As every husband knows, sometimes a wife can fiddle faster that a man can dance.

Jayme could not have been more professional, but I could tell that she was not quite sure of what to make of me being not quite sure of what to make of being on her show. I guess I was supposed to be delighted to be chosen, but as a 67 year old retiree living my dream life in Naples, Florida, the last thing I needed was to be making a fool of myself on national television. Most of the other segments of this eight-part series had been real tearjerkers. There had been six prior episodes, and some of those people had been through some terrible ordeals. My story was chosen as a military tribute for Veterans Day, and it too, was somewhat of a tear jerker. But I certainly wasn't going through tough times. Unless you include one of the worst stock market declines in history, a total collapse of the real estate market, the big three auto makers on the brink of disaster, and the implosion of the financial industry. Other than those minor annoyances, and the four stents in my coronary arteries, I was on top of the world.

The story I had written was not about me, but a wounded soldier I had picked up on a combat mission. I knew very well that when I turned it over to a TV producer that I would no longer be in control of it, or my life, for that matter. She was the production manager, the editor and the boss. I had no idea what to expect. I was just fodder for one of their NBC cannons. They had already been referring to me as Captain Bud Willis, and I hadn't been a Captain since coming off active duty in 1968. I rationalized that I was there for only one purpose; to honor the American soldiers and their families who had paid the ultimate sacrifice for our right to live in freedom, and to vote for whomever we wanted. And this is exactly what the country had done, just five days ago, in electing Barack Obama as the Commander in Chief of our Armed Forces, and the 44th President of the United States. These were wild historic times. The least I could do was to toss my little 500-word story into the grinder. A soldier's tribute on Veterans Day should be more than worth the personal inconvenience and uncertainty. At least, according to my wife!

Alex, the sound man at NBC, was putting a small microphone on my jacket lapel as the camera crew prepared to shoot the interview. My pulse quickened slightly. I looked around the small taping room. It had a low ceiling that needed painting, and felt like one of those multipurpose, basement-type rooms that had evolved over time. It was full of dated furniture among the state-of-the-art cameras and sound equipment. There was an old brown leather sofa, which I imagined could serve as a place for short naps during the "long hours of tedious boredom, interrupted by moments of stark terror," that must describe the life of the camera crew. The sofa was pushed up against the door of a small refrigerator, and had to be scooted out if someone wanted a bottle of water. I knew that old sofa had greater status than the refrigerator. I also knew that, for me to have noticed that minutia, my senses were on high alert mode.

"Look right at me, and pay no attention to the camera." Jayme instructed. Here we go! It took less than thirty minutes to shoot the film of me tell-reading the story. But that was preceded by a 20 minute wait for the fan on the HVAC to be turned off so it wouldn't interfere with the sound. This involved finding the man in charge of the fan. He had to be tracked down by cell phone, somewhere else in the NBC building, in another room, with another napping sofa. As I said earlier, part of the charm of life is that we all make

mistakes. Jayme directed my every move as though she already had the end result playing in her head. I, as usual, did not have a clue. The whole thing took less than an hour, and I was back in the hotel lobby. Jayme would take the film and edit it for the live show, which would take place at 10 am on Thursday, two days later. I would see it when the rest of the world did, and not before.

The desk clerk at the hotel had found a room for us. Someone at NBC had no doubt made a phone call after I told Jayme that her "VIP" had to get dressed in the men's spa. A major part of what we had come to New York to do was finished. Now, we had two days to enjoy free time in the city that never sleeps.

Our trip to the Big Apple is a story within a story, and it plays an important role in steering you to that very important pinpoint of light. It also helps to solve the problem of giving the reader a better idea about who "I" is in the current sense. That should make Mike Steinberg happy. Now, I can enjoy being in my stories as both a 67 year old and as a young boy. I will come back to this New York experience more than once, so hang in there.

Introduction Of The Main Characters

Most good stories start at the beginning.
  Indian proverb

Long before there were iPhones, Blackberries, microwave ovens, or lap top computers, there was a little village at the end of a dirt road in Middle Tennessee called Bluestocking Hollow. Bluestocking was the home of the Drydens. There were blackberries, of course, but they grew in thickets so dense the bears had to be especially hungry to go after them. This was rugged, rural early America.

In the complicated recipe that makes us who we are, the rootstock is the basic ingredient. No decent wine comes from poor grapes. For that reason, I can be grateful that I have a generous helping of Dryden in me. In the make-up of any living creature it is also not possible to deny the influence of terroir, the actual dirt from which it sprang. Some people believe that it's harder to know who you are and where you are going, if you don't know where you came from. "Place" has a way of defining us, and that place for me is Bluestocking Hollow, where my mother was born and raised.

You could never accuse these Drydens of Bluestocking of being quitters. They were a hearty clan of gritty survivors. If they started something they finished it. They were of Scottish heritage… slightly built, mild-mannered, honest, soft spoken and hard working. They held steadfast to the notion that people define their fate by the choices they make. *"There are no victims, only volunteers."* To this rule they were hardliners. They did not tolerate whiners within the ranks. If they married someone, they honored the vow, for better or for worse. They were loyal to their beliefs and to their kin.

The Drydens were part of the original group of settlers of Bedford County, Tennessee, and except for a genetic predisposition to heart problems, which they passed along to me; they were as tough as pine knots. The closest school was a one room school house in a nearby village called Pleasant Grove. All grades, 1 through 12 attended, and that was where my mother, Margaret Dryden, and her four siblings were educated. After she graduated she attended a nearby business college close to Nashville. She was quickly employed, and became a valuable office administrator for a food broker. Since she was able to purchase an automobile after only a couple of years of employment, it was generally agreed that this was quite an achievement for a working young lady in 1927. In two years time, at age 23, she would fall in love and marry the Bedford County man that would father me and all her children. This wedding took place on the third day of March in 1929, six months before the Great Depression.

There is a small graveyard in Bluestocking Hollow called Moore's Chapel Cemetery. That country graveyard is where my mother wanted to be buried, and she got her wish. She was placed close to her mom and dad. She had hoped that this would not happen in the winter when the ground was cold because she didn't like the idea of being buried in the frozen ground. She hated to be cold. But, she didn't catch a break there, because there was snow on the ground in Bluestocking Hollow on the first of April, 1971, and a bitter wind was blowing. Mama was survived by five sons, four daughters, and eight grandchildren. She requested her favorite hymn be sung, and she did get that wish, too. We sang every word of it:

On a hill far away stood an old rugged cross

An emblem of suffering and shame

How I loved that old cross where the dearest and best

And a world of lost sinners was saved.

So I'll cherish that old rugged cross

Til my trophies at last I lay down

I will cling to the old rugged cross

And exchange it someday for a crown.

If anyone on this earth ever deserved a crown, it would be Margaret. And hers would be smothered with jewels.

The Willis Clan

Everyone born into this world has dual citizenship
in the kingdom of the well and the kingdom of the sick.
    Susan Sontag

In a different part of Bedford County, which may have been considered Marshall County then, lived another family of hearty Tennessee pioneers with the surname Willis. The name Willis is a Welsh patronymic, which originally took the form Fitz Wille (son of Wille) until the Welsh began to drop the Fitz in favor of the final "s."

This group came from England by way of Virginia, and they were the descendants of William Willis. His great grandson, Alby, married Cynthia Jane Adeline Pinkney Glenn (1868-1977), and they produced ten children. The ninth of these was my father, Burr Willis (1904-1977), nicknamed Pete. There was a family history of health issues among the Willis clan too, but it wasn't necessarily heart related. It had more to do with alcohol, which was usually present when the men got together. Some of those Willis brothers seemed to turn to a dark side when they drank, displaying mean-spirited, abusive personality traits. Young Pete had been exposed to his share of odd behavior from male role models, but he didn't seem to be affected by it prior to meeting his future bride.

These two pioneering families were to be joined together on March 3rd, 1929, through the marriage of my father and my mother, Burr (Pete) Willis and Margaret Louise Dryden. A little more than a year later, on 12 April, 1930, they had the first of their nine children, Horace White Willis, my oldest brother.

So begins our story of an American family, my very own; alcohol, heart problems, warts and all. Some would say it is a tragic tale of two young lovers, bombarded by the Depression and overwhelmed by financial circumstances and their own human frailties. Others might see a courageous, battered, single mother struggling to overcome her shame and poverty to raise her children with dignity and honor. It is certainly a collection of human stories about very human people, told with lighthearted humor. Mostly, it's a story of survival; the constant motion of feet, hands, and arms that instinctively drives living creatures to their eventual outcome, for better or for worse; the discovery of life through the process of living it, rather than watching it happen.

Mr. and Mrs. Thomas Floyd Dryden

announce the marriage of their daughter

Margaret Louise

to

Mr. Burr Willis

on Sunday, March the third

Nineteen hundred and twenty-nine

Shelbyville, Tennessee

New York City

November 13, 2008, 8:30 am

"Unbelievable. Come over here and look at this." I was looking out the window of our seventh floor hotel room at three camels standing in the middle of Rockefeller Center. My wife, Lee, was fiddling with her small box of earrings and brought it with her to the window.

"It looks like the Arabs have arrived to purchase New York."

Lee and I live in a place called Tuscany Reserve in Naples, Florida, and a group of investors from the Arab Emirates had just purchased our development from our bankrupt homebuilder. The Arab jokes had been flying ever since.

Lee looked like a million dollars getting dressed for our television debut. We had a live segment to shoot that was to be complemented by the film that Jayme and I had made two days before. In another 2 or 3 hours we could put this whole thing in the rear view mirror, and get back to our normal life.

We didn't know what those camels were doing there, but we assumed it was for one of the many promotions that the TODAY show has to come up with every day to remain the top rated TV show in the nation. GE owns NBC, and the joke was going around that GE had to sell the "G," and now they were down to just an "E". GE stock had lost three quarters of its value during the brutal market decline.

"The black ones or the gold ones?" she asked, holding one earring up to each ear.

Lee doesn't know it, but she always says her first choice first, and her alternate last, so without even thinking I chose the black ones. "*I think so, too,*" she said.

I had learned from years of staying in hotels to look out the window to see how people on the street were dressed. This is a handy little piece of information to have when you're more than a thousand miles north of Naples in November. This is how I noticed the camels. In 15 minutes a guy named David would be coming to escort us to the NBC News Building. He would meet us in the lobby at 8:45am, a full hour and 45 minutes before the live show would be televised. They left nothing to chance. If there was going to be a snafu, they wanted plenty of time to fix it. Jayme had first phoned me back in September, so I had been waiting a couple of months for my 15 minutes of fame, or shame, depending on how it turned out. As I stared down on the city streets, most of my attention was focused on a handful of pigeons grazing on the sidewalk on the corner of 51st Street. Birds seem to be driven by a single purpose: food... as though every second of their existence depends on it. The herky-jerky movements of these New York pigeons fascinated me. Their feet were constantly in motion and their heads bobbed like chickens. Every few steps they found something to peck on the concrete. What could they possibly be finding to eat down there dodging all those swinging human feet? There must be better places in the city to find breakfast than on a concrete slab. They had wings... why didn't they use them? At least go find a Starbucks. Someone must have tossed out a bagel there, and they kept coming back to the memory of it. Birdbrains!

Distractions like this were part of the reason I never became a billionaire, but I wasn't complaining. I had pecked around on my share of concrete slabs in the securities business, and stored up enough bagels to be living the good life in sunny Florida.

My six years since retirement had been a reflective time for me, and those pigeons reminded me of the way my family had to survive. I was thinking about my book, and that single speck of light that represented the purpose of it. If only life was that simple. If those birds can turn their frenetic pecking into a driving cause, why can't I seem to find a single pinpoint of light for my book's existence? Maybe the pigeons were analogous to my own family. We were the tail end of the pecking order, and we had to show up every day, and keep our feet moving in order to survive. Peck, peck, peck... you never know what you might find on the sidewalk.

But showing up every day may not always be a good thing. Ernest Hemingway used to hand-hunt those pigeons when he was a starving writer in Paris. He carried a few kernels of corn to lure them into his clutch, and then he discretely wrung their necks, stuffed them in his jacket, and took them home to cook for lunch. There's a quirky metaphor in there somewhere.

Bluestocking Hollow

There is something about getting up at five in the morning to feed the chickens and milk the cows that gives one a lifelong perspective on the price of butter and eggs.
  William E. Vaughan

It's hard to imagine my mother without children, but not so hard to imagine her as a child. It was easy to get her to talk about her childhood. She never shared much with her children about her single life as an adult. Her fondest memories seemed to be of that little one room schoolhouse in Bluestocking. She still remembered the names of her teachers and some of the "long, tall strollups" and "stand-up-in-the-corners" that attended school with her. Slow learners made an impression on her, but the winters seemed to have made the biggest impression. She was not a fan of cold weather. The teacher apparently depended on the older boys in the class to start the fire in the pot bellied stove before the girls and young kids arrived. Sometimes that didn't get done in time, and the day got off to a pretty raw start until everybody got warmed up.

One of the older, semi-literate, male students was particularly challenged in the spelling department according to one of her stories. One winter day the teacher had to interrupt the spelling class to go outside and fetch some fuel for the fire. (They used wood to get the fire started and coal to keep it going.) As soon as the teacher closed the door behind him, the overzealous teenaged student, caught up in the excitement of learning to spell, blurted out the letters, "B-R-C... Mr. Brown went out the door to get some coal." These three letters, apparently, were supposed to spell that entire sentence, according to him. This was riotous to the younger kids in the room, and the story became a schoolyard classic. The memory of this simple tale brought great pleasure to this woman for the rest of her life. These were farm children, and they all shared the chores of farm life. School took a backseat to both planting time and harvest time, so school was out most of the summer. This custom was important then but a ridiculous waste of time and resources now, but don't tell the teachers that.

Margaret had a quiet mystery about her. As a little boy, it was fascinating to me to hear her childhood stories and think about what made this woman tick. Hers seemed to be a more simple time, with stories about butter and eggs, cows and chickens. The gentle way she told these tales made me feel sleepy, even in the middle of the day.

Although he died before I was born, her father Thomas Dryden, was reputed to be a kind- hearted, generous man who was good to his children. He led more by example than with an iron hand. This created an atmosphere in his home of calm security, which made young people feel safe, if not downright warm and cozy. His wife, who survived him by 35 years, was a great cook, especially when it came to cakes and pies. Her house always smelled just like a bakery. We came to know this woman as Granny (seen milking a cow on the front of the book). In addition to milking cows and making butter, she was not adverse to wringing a chicken's neck for Sunday dinner, and asking the kids to help with the easy part, plucking it. This was done by pouring boiling water over the headless bird which made the feathers easier to pull out. She liked to astonish children with this Sunday chicken ritual, partly to show that farm life was not for the faint of heart, and partly because she knew they would never forget the memory of it. She was absolutely right about both those things. Granny was a woman who knew her part and did it well. Margaret inherited these same traits from her mother.

Love In Bluestocking Hollow

A man normally falls in love with a woman
who asks the kind of questions that he can answer.
        Ronald Coleman

Nobody alive today knows how Burr (Pete) Willis and my future mother got together. Perhaps they first met at the annual Bedford County Muster day. This was a day when all families got together in order for the men, both young and old, to account for themselves for military service, if needed. It was the highlight of the year. They usually made a party out of it with target shooting, music, wrestling matches, and plenty of food and dancing. Margaret was a paragon of virtue at 22, in 1928, had a good job and an automobile. As a single woman, she had a good life going with her family in Bluestocking, but she left all that to get married to a man she had known less than a year.

The Depression managed to take its toll on the Dryden family farm in Bluestocking. Then, when family genetic history reared its ugly head, and Thomas Dryden died of a heart attack at age 54, they were unable to hang on to the farm. Had Margaret remained a single working girl, she might have been able to help with some of the family finances; instead, she had already chosen a different route. The family lost their revered home place, and by then, my mother had three hungry mouths tugging at her apron. Margaret may have had some guilt about her decisions. Her circumstances certainly were not contributing to the overall financial conundrum. But, to her, and all the Drydens, there was a simple code, *"you get what you get because you did what you did."*

This rugged, rural life in Bedford County was the only thing that we knew for sure that Margaret and Pete had in common. Pete was the youngest of six brothers, and he had four sisters. They say he was the family "favorite" and had lots of charm, plenty of wit and charisma. Everybody liked Pete, according to his youthful reputation. He was, apparently, the quintessential country boy. He got along well with his new father-in-law, and they respected each other during their short relationship.

When Pete's father-in-law, Thomas Dryden, died in 1937, Pete insisted that his 5 year old daughter, Martha, attend the funeral. Small children didn't normally go to funerals in those days, but Pete knew that his daughter had a close relationship with the deceased man, and he wanted her to have closure with her friend. He even held her up to view her grandfather and told his little girl some nice stories about him. Whatever his motive might have been, this made a lasting impression on a 5 year old. So, our daddy had a way about him… a certain *je ne sais quoi*, to steal a phrase from the French, meaning "I don't know what" or "hard to put your finger on it." Anyway, whatever he had was good enough for my mother, who was the other half of the puzzle. They were married at Moore's Chapel in Bluestocking six months before the October Crash of 1929. Not exactly the best timing or the ideal economic environment for raising a young family!

After their marriage, Pete maintained a close relationship with all his five brothers and four sisters in Marshall County and visited them often, usually by himself. During the Depression, and for several years afterwards, he found it difficult to find good, steady work that paid the bills. He had several obstacles in his path: the sour economy, WW II didn't help things, and every couple of years he had a new mouth to feed. He held a variety of jobs in a number of towns around Middle Tennessee from 1930 to 1942, moving his growing family nearly a dozen times. The Tennessee birthplaces of his children provide some clues to his job struggles: Lawrenceburg, Gallatin, Shelbyville, Columbia, and most notably, Tullahoma, where most of his children spent the majority of their formative years.

Pete finally settled into the grocery business as a meat market manager, or butcher, as they were called in those days. This was a natural transition for men who were raised on a farm and paid attention to all the things that went on there. Pete would have had plenty of mentors with five older brothers. They would have slaughtered a hog and a steer at least once a year, and shared the chores of processing them. Where Pete went to school, or if he went, was never revealed to me, but I do know that he did have an intelligent mind and a gift for math, which was a big help to him in the grocery business.

Pete had an older brother named Alby, who was nicknamed John. John and his oldest son, John Harlan Willis (1921-1945), had an argument over a sensitive family matter that caused John Harlan to leave home and join the Navy. The story of how this 21 year old received the Medal of Honor at the battle of Iwo Jima is one of the most heroic war stories of WWII, and deserves its own section later in this book. There are as many as 28 memorials honoring John Harlan including the USS John Willis, a Naval Destroyer named for him. The highest military honor is usually awarded posthumously, and such was the case with John Harlan. Alby's loss of a magnificent son, stemming from a family argument, is a testament to the dysfunction that surrounded the Willis clan.

The relationship between the Willis family and the Drydens was congenial, but   socializing between the two groups was rare, if it happened at all. Pete apparently kept his wife and children at arm's length from his brothers and sisters, and seemed to want a separate personal life. For all his alleged charisma, I don't remember ever meeting one of his friends. I do remember one of my daddy's older brothers, Tott, making a cameo appearance at our house in Tullahoma with his family, when I was seven or eight years old. He was a big, affable man with a round, reddish brown face and a very outgoing, sweet wife who was a little squirrelly. I have since learned that Tott was just about the only one of those brothers that didn't have a "mean streak."

My memory of the Drydens was exactly the opposite of all that. We visited them regularly at Thanksgiving and Christmas. I never visited any of the Willis family. Pete and Margaret, the odd couple, would produce 9 living children over the next 18 years, and I was number six.

That background will be important as we see how these hands will eventually be played out. There is a saying that I have used over the years to help explain why certain people suddenly exhibit odd behavior traits that seem to come out of nowhere. *"If a card is in the deck, sooner or later, it must be played."* I tend to agree with those people who like to like to know where they came from.

CHILDREN OF PETE AND MARGARET WILLIS, DATES AND PLACES OF BIRTH, ALL IN TENNESSEE

Horace White Willis, born 12 April 1930 in Shelbyville

Martha Willis, born 3 January, 1932 in Shelbyville

Virginia Ann Willis, born 3 October, 1933 in Columbia

Tommy Willis, born 24 April, 1936 in Shelbyville

Sara Marie Willis, born 11 June, 1938 in Lawrenceburg

Beasley Willis (Buddy/Bud), born 2 September, 1941 in Galatin

Paschal Willis (Tykie), born 25 September, 1943 in Shelbyville

James Dryden Willis (Jimmy/Beau), born 2 January, 1945 in Shelbyville

Linda Gail Willis, born 20 February, 1947 in Tullahoma

Although Mother had nine children, they seemed to come in three different packages. This is the way I will attempt to tell their stories:

Horace (1930), Martha (1932), and Ann (1934) ...The Depression Era

Tommy(1936), Sara (1938), and Buddy (1941) … The Fifties Era

Tykie (1943), Beau (1945), and Linda (1947) ... The Boomer Era

PART I - THE DEPRESSION ERA

All great things are accomplished under adverse circumstances.
Nick Saban

Number One Son, Horace

If the oldest child in the family is supposed to be the leader, Mama's fist-born did not disappoint. He carried our banner high and turned out to be our go-to-guy in almost every emergency situation. He was the closest thing we had to 911. If one of the little ones cut themselves on a broken milk bottle, Horace knew how to make a butterfly bandage so that it wouldn't need stitches or leave a scar. In the absence of a responsible father who normally would have done that sort of thing, Horace was exemplary. Where he learned it, I have no clue.

As a young boy, and the first child, he would have had the greatest exposure to both sides of our family tree in those early years. Horace was probably the only one of Margaret's children that might have actually remembered very much about the Dryden home in Bluestocking, or would have spent any meaningful time with Pete's family in Marshall County. He would also be the most likely one to know the names of some of the places where Pete had to move his family in order to find work during those Depression-era years, because he would have been dragged along to every one of them. But Pete finally settled his family in Tullahoma, Tennessee, a little town full of remarkable people who eventually would help raise his family in his absence. Tullahoma is smack dab in the middle of the 600-mile-long state of Tennessee, 72 miles southeast of Nashville and 60 miles north of Huntsville, Alabama. It is still, today, one of the friendliest places you will ever find.

Tullahoma was a sleepy little railroad town until WWII, when it received a huge economic boost as an indirect result of a letter that Albert Einstein wrote to President Roosevelt in 1939. American scientists had information that the Germans were attempting to build an extremely destructive bomb out of Uranium 235. FDR created the Manhattan Project in an attempt to beat them to the punch. The secret plan involved using small rural areas that weren't obvious military targets. Tennessee had plenty of small rural towns as well as strong Congressional clout, and Oak Ridge was selected as the cornerstone of this well-funded, government science project, the Atom Bomb.

A couple of years later, rural Tullahoma was selected as the site for a massive Army training camp called Camp Forrest. A large wooded area was quickly converted into an 85,000 acre military fortress that would train hundreds of thousands of troops. The recently completed Tennessee Valley Authority provided plenty of water and electricity and all the ingredients came together. The population of Tullahoma exploded from 6,500 to over 75,000 during this war-time period and it was considered somewhat of a boom- town as well as a vacation destination. More than 25,000 POW's were also housed there during WWII.

After 1945, Tullahoma changed dramatically. The buildings at Camp Forrest were auctioned off, and dismantled right down to the foundations of the buildings. The only things left were the concrete foundation slabs and a few stone chimneys. When all the soldiers moved out, the town returned to normal...no more boom-town. Camp Forrest became nothing more than a huge parking place for teenagers, and the deserted, paved roads turned into late-night drag racing strips. But, during its heyday, sometime in 1943, Daddy found work in Tullahoma as a butcher in Bill Jones's grocery store.

Pete was a hard working man, but by the time his oldest son was a teenager, Pete had cultivated quite a few drinking buddies. Tullahoma had a reputation as a party town, because of all those soldiers in the area, and this was not necessarily a good thing for a man with Pete's gregarious personality.

Horace was old enough to help his daddy at the store occasionally, and could see the changes in his father's behavior. Pete was becoming a classic Jekyll and Hyde. He had apparently inherited the gene that steered his value system toward alcohol, and he was developing a chemical addiction to it. This was not an uncommon trait in the Willis family, but that was not the worst of it. When he drank he took on an abusive disposition.

In his prime, Pete had a sharp mind, and as a butcher, he had the uncanny ability to hold a piece of meat in his hand and estimate its weight and the price of it in his head, almost to the penny, before placing it on the scales. But weighing his grocery skills against his growing annoying behavior was no contest. The entire family was tiptoeing on eggshells around this weak-minded bully. Horace could only watch, as his father would turn on the charm for a customer and suddenly switch to show contempt for a family member, almost as if he resented having a wife and children. He had also been abusive to our sweet mother for some time, and this was tearing Horace into little pieces. One didn't have to have a psychology degree to know that this was far from normal behavior. When Pete did come home, late, and worn out from working all day and drinking afterwards, he ordered everyone to go to bed no matter what time it was. He insisted on Mother lying with him. The older girls would literally have to hide under their bed with a flashlight to get their homework done.

In sharp contrast, Horace, now 17, was beginning to shape his own adult values, and had set some very high standards for himself. He had an active social life with plenty of friends. He played football, and was a popular dance partner on the high school party circuit. This post war period was an era of high ideals for all Americans, and Pete didn't seem to be getting with the program. Horace must have been anguished and disgusted from watching his 40 year old father being diminished into the tormenting bully that he had become. Alcoholism was prevalent in those days, but it was not recognized as a disease like it is today. It was just considered voluntary insanity, and unacceptable.

There was no way for the rest of us to know how long all the resentment had been festering inside Horace, but he was not about to allow his abusive, foulmouthed father, to ruin his life, or to bully his mother and younger sisters. This would not do. He had seen enough. Pete was about to find out that he was not the only person in the family who could cop an attitude, and that he certainly didn't have a monopoly on anger.

The Intervention

Bravery is the ability to perform properly even when you are scared half to death.
> Omar Bradley

The exact day is not certain, but I know that Horace was 17, and Mother had just brought home her ninth bundle of joy to our ramshackled rental house at 701 Jefferson Street in Tullahoma. Linda Gail Willis was about two weeks old, having been born on Feb. 20, 1947. It was in the dead of winter, and there was a frozen base of snow on the ground. It was bitter cold, both outside and inside our house. Darkness came early that night, and with it, a tension settled in the house, as though the barometric pressure was dropping sharply. It felt like a tornado was brewing. Even as a toddler, I could tell that things were far from normal that night. It seemed like hours passed, while we all waited stressfully for Daddy to come home. It didn't have to be said, and it wasn't, but something far from ordinary was about to happen.

Horace and Mama waited and talked in the back bedroom of the house while the rest of us huddled in the front of the house, the door closed between us. There was a coal stove in the room which provided adequate heat when we had coal and someone to tend it, but I don't remember much heat coming from it that night. Finally, Daddy came home, and entered through the back door of the house, where Horace was waiting.

The fact that we did not own a gun was a good thing for all of us, especially Daddy. Instead, Horace tried to explain to this inebriated man that if he could not come home sober, and treat his wife and children with more respect, then he would not be welcome there any longer. The child had become father of the man. The bully, of course, became furious, which must have been terrifying to his young son. But, as with most bullies, he was no match for a determined, well prepared champion of justice, especially when the bully was drunk. Our young hero was indeed prepared and fit, both mentally and physically. Newsreels from the recent war victory had bolstered the fighting spirit of all young American "warriors," and right now, Horace was on the front line for his family. He was fighting for freedom from our own brand of tyranny.

We could hear the sounds of a struggle; the scuffling of feet and furniture. The ass- kicking could not have taken more than a couple of minutes, but they were the longest two minutes in history. It seemed like forever. The scene on our side of the door could mostly be described as big eyes and brown shorts. The youngsters in the room eyed the older sisters for clues as to what was going on in there, until we realized that they didn't know any more than two week old Linda did. The loud thumping and scuffling noises would stop, and start again. Martha was armed with a piece of stove wood, just in case she might be pressed into service. Suddenly it was quiet. We heard a screen door slam shut. We all looked around the room at each other as though this might honestly be the last time we would ever see each other. We stared back at the door, not knowing when it would open or who would walk through.

Finally, it happened. The door opened and there stood Horace. It was like a cowboy movie where the good guy wins but nobody gets killed. He wasn't even bloody. Horace stood 10 feet tall that night.

The relief in that room was so great, that I swear it must have sucked oxygen through the stove flue and rekindled the fire. The house got warmer. Horace got some coal from somewhere, and made us a big fire with Martha's weapon. Things got nice and toasty warm. The little ones had to go to bed. The girls did their homework without having to crawl under the bed. Nobody said very much of anything for the rest of the evening. This was all just another night in Mama's helter-skelter world, but I could have sworn that I heard giggling that night between Martha and Ann. Everybody in that house knew, that, for better or for worse, our lives would never be the same after that night.

The next morning we awoke to a quiet house. Apparently, lying out there face down in the snow, Daddy didn't feel like going back in the house and strapping on any more of Horace. Pete was strong and physical, but Horace...well, he was fighting for a higher purpose. Daddy probably sought whatever it was that got him in that position to begin with, because he didn't come back home that night. He probably had a warm place to go since there was plenty of evidence that he had his share of lady friends, according to stories we would hear later. I do know this: nobody felt sorry for him.

He didn't come back the next night either, or the next, or the next week. Some nights we could hear crunching footsteps in the snow, and our antennae would tingle, "Daddy?"

A change came over all of us during those next couple of weeks. Even in my pre-kindergarten brain I could tell that we were all growing closer. We weren't just a lump entity of Willis kids anymore. Each one of us was a real, individual person, and somehow I knew that we would all be better off because of what had happened. The biggest problem was that we didn't have a penny to our names.

After a few more weeks, the fear went away, and that was the last I ever saw of that brutal man. He never came back. Some say he went to Toledo, Ohio to live with some relatives. There were sightings from time to time. The curious thing to me was that he never even came back for any of his things. Years later, we would hear from Pete's brothers and sisters that we "ran him off," which is a ridiculous notion, of course. We would have loved to have had a caring, sober father. But no family needs what he was bringing home. Pete failed to tell his siblings that he had become an abusive, womanizing alcoholic, and they, of course, wanted to believe the best about him.

We didn't see as much of Horace after that either, but not for the same reason. It seems that Horace had made a decision, and now he had to back it up. *Those damned choices again!* Within a few days he had dropped out of high school to take a job. Our brave 17 year old was the bread winner now.

Our landlord on Jefferson Street was a notorious bootlegger, and one of our father's drinking buddies. Whatever arrangement he had made for us to live in that house on Jefferson Street terminated with Daddy's departure. It was only a month or so before we were sent packing. Understandably, I suppose, since we had no means to pay the rent. Even a five year old knew that much about economics. Trying to imagine what that must have been like for Mama is almost impossible. Horace was barely 17 years old, with two years of high school left. My oldest sister Martha was 15, Ann was close behind her at 14. Then there was Tommy, 11, Sara, 9, and I was almost 6, Tykie 4, Jimmy was 2 and Linda was 2 months.

Just about everybody in town knew part of our story by now. News travels fast in a small town, especially through the Tullahoma school system. I'm sure it touched many of them. But they didn't know the whole story. In fact, none of us knew the whole story. It would not have been in Mama's nature to tell anyone of the constant abuse that took place under our roof for so many years, and no one was more ashamed of it than her. Nor did the older children share their sad experiences about Daddy. All those things became dark secrets, and ultimately part of the code. The "Code of Silence," as it has come to be known, the holy grail of the alcoholic family.

In the future we would not be allowed to discuss that incident, our father's behavior, or any negative issues of the past in great detail if we ever mentioned them at all. Instead, we were advised to keep our eyes planted firmly onto our future. Therefore, any attempt on my part to tell any of these stories, is to tell only a child's version. The only one who really knew everything was Mama. And she never told anyone anything.

She is also the only person who would know where the support came from to get us through the months ahead. We still woke up every day to a cold house and a full agenda that needed to be managed, and Mama still had hungry mouths to feed. Perhaps Daddy's old grocer boss realized that Pete had left his family bereft, and he was the one who helped find us a small house in town. We don't know. We do know that Mama paid a visit to the Red Cross office to seek advice. What they told her is anybody's guess. Her three brothers in Shelbyville may have helped. At any rate, within six weeks, we moved, or I should say, we walked to our new home.

Early Memories

Memory is a way of holding on to the things you love. Who you are,
And the things you never want to lose.
> *The Wonder Years*

Horace's dramatic intervention with our father took place at 701 Jefferson Street in Tullahoma. My two older sisters, Martha and Ann, were far more emotionally involved in that episode than the six clueless adolescents in the room. Things might have taken a much different turn if Daddy had come through that door and Martha had been called into action with her trusty piece of stove-wood. The thought of that makes me shutter and chuckle at the same time. Thank God it didn't come to that. My memories of that humble residence are few and far between, but since they are some of my most vivid early memories, I am including some of them for my own simple amusement. As I said, Mama had three sets of children, and some of us were too young at that time to be living in the real world, but we still had memories.

Life on Jefferson Street seemed pretty normal to this five year old boy, just hanging out with Mama while she took care of the three "little ones." The older siblings were usually in school, so everybody pretty much left me alone, and I had no complaints. When school was out, there was plenty of laughing and cutting up among the older siblings and some of their friends who were always around. I mostly watched, and took mental notes about how my life would be later on. The schools and neighborhoods in the South were segregated in the Forties, but somebody forgot to tell us. Some of our best play pals were black people, and they lived just across the street from us. Their daddy was an electrician, and he fixed all of Mama's electrical problems, and never charged her a penny. We played together all the time. Curiously, we could go over in their yard to play but their mother wouldn't allow them to come over in our yard for some reason.

After school, when the older kids came home, there was a lot of insider stuff going on with Mama and the girls. Far too complicated for a preschooler! At Christmas time I would cut Santa Claus pictures out of the paper. I collected them and carefully kept them in a King Edward cigar box. I would take them out and study them or try to count them. The number 27 comes to mind. To this day, the smell of a cheap cigar reminds me of Christmas.

Sometimes in the afternoon, Mama and I would have the house all to ourselves when the little ones were asleep and the others were in school. She would try to entertain me, by giving me a little something to do while she was cooking or folding clothes. Of course, it wouldn't take me long before I bungled it. But she never scolded me. She didn't like to fuss at her children. I might be asked to walk up to Scott's grocery on the corner, and pick up an item for cooking. She had a way of making even the smallest one of us feel like we were making some sort of contribution.

On weekends, I occasionally got included in some adventures with my sister Sara, who was three years older than me. Sara liked to stretch her boundaries, and literally "push the envelope." She saw each compass heading as a new challenge.

There was a frontier out there, and she wanted to explore it. On these adventures, she would walk a little further up, or down, the street than the day before, until she was comfortable knowing what was out there, and that she could find her way back home. This was never more than a few blocks in any one direction, but in the mind of an 8 year old, this was an ingenious way of stretching the comfort zone. Maybe Mama told Sara that I was her responsibility, I'm not sure, but she never bullied me. She always took me under her wing, and I always felt safer when she was around. If she ever cried I didn't know about it. She just seemed tougher than any girl that I had ever seen. For me, those adventure hikes were scary, and I will have to admit, being out of sight of our house scared the devil out of me. It seemed like every other house had a big, barking dog tied up (or not) in the yard, and most of them seemed bigger than me. I wasn't ready to run with the big dogs and felt safer at home on the porch. If it wasn't for those yappy dogs we might still be getting mail, milk and newspapers delivered to the front door.

The older girls had some real friendly high school boyfriends that would come by our house on the weekends. They would park their car on the street in front of the house, and the girls would come out, and they would all sit around on the hood, the trunk, or the running boards. The car had a handle coming out of the front grill, which they used to start the car by giving it a sharp crank. The first time I wandered out to see what all the fuss was about, I expected to be shooed away immediately. Instead, the girls just introduced me. The guys would always ask which number I was. I thought they meant my age, so I held up 5 fingers. I barely knew what numbers were, much less what that question meant, but the girls answered for me and told them that I was number six. From then on the boys just called me "Number Six." None of them ever ran me off, but they didn't ask me to go for a spin with them either. One time, the boy who owned the car (I think his name was Howard Tucker) picked me up and sat me in the driver's seat, and asked me if I could drive. He put my hands on the wheel like he was showing me how the car worked. What a fun guy! If I got too comfortable out there, Mama would always call me in, like she needed me to help her in the house. Women must have a secret code.

My older brother Tommy was my male role model. He was about 10 or 11 when he took a dull, rusty hand saw and decided to climb the tree in the front yard and saw off the lower limb. It was no small limb, about 6 or 7 inches thick. He would saw it one direction until his arm got tired, which was often, and then he would face another direction and saw the other way. Somewhere in the process he must have forgotten where he was, because he ended up on the wrong side of the limb when it fell. This could have had a tragic ending, since Tommy had a flesh eating saw, as well as a long fall and a heavy limb to deal with. Everything turned out ok. He only had the breath knocked out of him, which gave him a few seconds to contemplate death. It was a good thing he wasn't hurt. You just could not take that story to the emergency room with a straight face. Mama couldn't even lecture him without laughing, and it took a few years for Tommy to outgrow that incredible boo-boo. We were all banned from tree climbing for awhile.

One of Tommy's friends taught us how to take a hammer and knock off a piece of asphalt in the street about the size of a piece of bubble gum, and chew it. Mama didn't go for that one either, but what's a role model for, if not to teach you cool stuff?

We had an ice box on the back porch, and the ice man would deliver ice to our house a couple of times a week during the summer. His morning arrival was a highly anticipated event. All the neighborhood kids tried to meet the ice truck, and we begged the ice man to give us a little chunk of ice to gnaw on. He always found a way to make that happen, without taking it off our little 25 pound block. His truck was a brown pickup which he parked in the shade of Tommy's oak tree. He carried several blocks of ice in the back with a tarpaulin spread over it to keep the burning sun off the ice. You wanted to be there when he came to the back of the truck, because when he flipped up that tarp, it was like winter was hiding under there. The cold blast only lasted a couple of seconds, but it was a good reward for standing barefoot on that melting asphalt. The tarp, the ice, the truck and the iceman all combined to create a musty bouquet, and all the ingredients needed to be there to get a whiff of it. He had big metal tongs for grabbing the ice, and then would swing it off the pickup onto his leg, and carry it to the back porch against his leg. He wore long leather chaps like a cowboy, to protect his leg from the ice. We all wanted to be the ice man, and he seemed to know that. No matter how many kids there were, he pretty much accommodated every one of us somehow. I couldn't help notice that some of the larger blocks of ice had the corners knocked off, and ours didn't. When men were nice to you, it really made you feel good. Our daddy wasn't the warm, fuzzy type.

I could tell that our iceman enjoyed having all those little kids make a big to-do over him. I think we added a little warmth to the ice man's life. I'll bet he went home and told his wife about us, and I'll bet it made her smile and give him a big hug. What better thing could he possibly have had to tell her about his work day? But I will also wager one other thing. I'll bet he rarely heard the words "thank you" from many of his other customers.

One of the few memories I have of my daddy happened at that house one Sunday afternoon after dinner (that's lunch on Sunday in the South). Daddy was spending a rare couple of hours at home during the summer before he hit the road. He played a game with me and my two little brothers. He had hidden some coins in the front yard, and he sat on the front porch and directed us to find them by telling us if we were hot or cold. I was about 5, and my two little brothers were 3 and less than 2 years old. Daddy was getting a little irritated that I was finding all the coins. Tykie and Jimmy (Beau) were just wandering around, not quite getting it. So he told me to stand still, until someone else got lucky. Now I'm just 5, and I'm thinking, "I just learned the game a few minutes ago, and these two goobers don't know the difference between hot and cold, so you better get them out of the yard before they step on a bee." How could I possibly have had more sense than a grown man at that moment? We all came away with a few pennies and nickels, which later I collected from my clueless little brothers, but it was a silly game. All we had to do is wait for him to go to sleep and sort through the handful of change he left of the dresser. We knew he never counted that.

Later, that same afternoon, my role model found a half pint of something under the claw foot bathtub where Daddy kept some stash. To say that Tommy tried some of it might be an understatement. The way Mama reacted, he must have *"got all up in it."* Anyway, between Daddy and Tommy, they found a way to suck most of the fun out of that Sunday.

***

The move from Jefferson Street took us about 30 minutes as I trailed along behind Mama and some of the others for the mile walk to town to our new home. The little row of shotgun houses behind a Pan Am gas station in downtown Tullahoma was not much different than a slave's quarters. There were three or four small white shacks that resembled some of my first grade artwork. We were to live in only one of them. It could not have contained more than 800 or 900 square feet of living space. And we were a family of 10.

The two teenage girls, Martha and Ann, slept in the tiny living room. There were cots for the in-betweeners, and the little ones slept with Mama, if she slept at all. I'm not sure where Horace slept. All of us shared a bathroom so small that the door could not be opened when someone else was standing or sitting in the room. Trying to get ready for school was comical. The big tree in the back yard was pretty handy for the boys, both morning and night. I hope we didn't kill it. Out of necessity, we had to train ourselves to use the bathroom at school. Later on, when the boys were old enough for P.E. classes, we learned the advantages of taking our showers at school as well. We never had a shower at home, only a bathtub. It usually looked liked the planet Saturn, with its multiple rings. You could say we had a small carbon footprint. Most of the little ones took their baths at the same time.

The only entertainment, other than ourselves, was the radio, and we played it night and day. We did have a nice Christmas there. Santa Claus really did come that year. Sometime during the night, someone left a large box of gifts on our front stoop. That was the year I figured out that there was no Santa Claus. Why were the presents on the front porch? What's up with that? Something didn't add up. Sara finally told me the big Santa secret, but asked me not to tell that I knew. I think this made her feel powerful to be able to transfer information as important as that to someone who didn't already know it. I guess I felt I had to be a hero too, and proceeded to immediately tell somebody else. That turned out to be a terrible decision, because it broke Tykie's little four-year-old heart when I blabbed it to him the next morning. He started crying, and I had to hide out for a while. This was Christmas morning…why did everything have to be so complicated?

In addition to the Tinker Toys, or whatever else was in that box on the porch, Mama had something for everybody. These were things she had put on layaway months ago. It was easier for her to walk to a store now that we lived in town. So while we were at school, she had time to make a Christmas for us. But it was a 12 month program, because shopping was not an easy thing for her for several reasons. First, it's hard to find quality Christmas gifts that are priced under a dollar. Secondly, she would not be alone when she shopped. She was never alone. Preschoolers dictated her every move and she did not have enough arms to carry all the people that needed to tag along.

Finding Our Way

What saves a man is to take a step. Then another step and another. It is always the same step but you have to take it.
    Antoine de Saint Exupery

Horace had been working part-time at a drug store and now had to seek full time employment to help pay the bills. He was hired by Morris Simon and Harry Hill of the Tullahoma News. The newspaper office was only a couple of blocks from our "slaves' quarters" in downtown Tullahoma. They were delighted to have a hard working 17 year old like my brother. There was no 40 hour work week back then, so Horace worked as many overtime hours as regular hours for no extra pay. The unspoken rule was "the job is to get the paper out, however long it might take." There was no union either, so the other rule was "closest to the broom sweeps." This meant that if something needed to be done, don't wait for somebody else to do it. Horace did practically every job in the place and was able to work his way up the ladder quickly. The printing was all done in-house. They melted their own lead and set their own type. Working around those heavy machines was dangerous work for a journeyman, let alone for a teenager like Horace. There were several occasions where Horace was badly burned by the hot lead or injured by those old printing presses, but nothing stopped the "paper." Lawyers would have had a heyday with that situation now, but it was commonplace then to work in hazardous places, and nobody thought anything about it. The Tullahoma News was printed twice a week, and if the presses broke down, everybody worked round the clock to get them ready for the next printing.

Sometimes Horace worked 24 or 36 hours without sleep. It was rare for him to come home before dawn on press night. He worked this job until he was 30 years old. In 1960, he was hired to run the print shop at Arnold Engineering Development Center in Tullahoma, where he worked for the next 25 years.

Martha

It has never been clear to me why rural people in those days had so many children.

Maybe it was like making biscuits. "While you have your hands in the dough, you may as well make a batch." I'm not complaining, these are my brothers and sisters I'm talking about, but country people seemed to apply the same logic that they used with their livestock, more is better. Production is the name of the game on the farm, and if a broodmare can be bred as early as two weeks after the birth of a foal, who are we to argue with nature? Nothing makes a mare happier that being pregnant. Likewise, if a cow is just standing around eating grass, it might as well be multi-tasking and making a calf at the same time. But whatever the reason, poor country people and large families seemed to go together in Mama's day, and she had three children smack in the middle of the Great Depression between 1930 and 1933. Times could not have been more difficult. What was she thinking, if anything? In a family that believed that everyone had to carry their own stack of bricks, she was taking on quite a load.

Her first three babies lived with a different mother, and with different circumstances than the rest of us. Firstly, for better or for worse, they saw more of their father. Secondly, raising kids didn't come with a complete set of instructions, so Mama was making it up as she went along. She had to get better with experience, so these first three were her "guinea pigs." Times could not have been worse economically, and the anxiety quotient had to be extreme at times.

To put it mildly, Horace, Martha and Ann most certainly grew up in a different world than the others.

The process of naming Margaret's children should have been an early warning signal that this family was living in Dysfunction Junction. When Martha was born, she was not given a middle name. This would be explained to us as being part of Pete's quirky personality. He didn't have a middle name, so somewhere along the way he decided that middle names were unnecessary. In addition, whether he was half serious or not, he jokingly disclaimed any of his children if they were born with blond hair. (Most of the Drydens were blond and most of the Willises had dark hair). However, if the child was born a brunette, he proudly claimed the honor of a naming it. (What a jerk!) The fact that this baby hair usually falls out in a few weeks and might be replaced with a completely different color did not seem to factor into his mindset. There were lots of Marthas on his side of the family, so he chose that name for his second child. Just Martha, no middle name! She was born a brunette and remained that way. I can't speak about any of the other Willis Marthas because I never knew them, but I think Pete got himself a jewel in this one. I think he thought so too, because he seemed to favor her.

One of my first memories of Martha goes back to Jefferson Street and, it illustrates her grit and sense of humor. It takes us back to that same little stove, where she armed herself for battle with that stick of stove wood. In the wintertime, we rarely got dressed in the bedroom because it was freezing. As soon as we got out from under the warm covers, we grabbed our clothes and made a bee line for the living room to get dressed, near the only stove in the house. We huddled around it as closely as we could get, in various stages of undress. (Modesty had not been invented yet.) When she was about 15 years old, she was clowning around while getting dressed, and when she bent over to step into her skirt, her butt touched the hot stove, and she *"screamed bloody murder."* Everyone laughed so hard that she had to laugh too, even though it melted her panties and took the skin off. That had to hurt like the devil, but she laughed her way though it with everybody else and went on to school like always. I wondered if she had to stand up most of the day.

Martha was the centerpiece of any family gathering and was the apple of her granddaddy Dryden's eye. She was only 5 when he had his fatal heart attack in 1937, but she still remembers pleasant stories with him calling her to his rocking chair to chat with him when she was only 3 or 4 years old. He was a doting grandparent, and missed having little ones around the house. Horace, Martha and Ann spent considerable time with the Drydens in Bluestocking, and they had to live with their grandparents for interim periods when our daddy was looking for hard-to-find jobs, which seemed to be most of the time.

THE PAN AM

From March 1947 until the summer of 1949, we occupied that ridiculous little house in downtown Tullahoma. During that time I finished my first and second year of school at South Jackson Elementary School. The house was directly behind a "filling station," and they stored their old tires in the back of the station about 12 feet from our little house. The big round, white sign on the corner with the blue letters told us it was a Pam Am full service gas station. The stack of old tires made a great playground, and we were about the same color as the tires most of the summer until Mama made the tires off limits. They also dumped the oil from the oil changes back there. They just poured it on the ground. It was an environmental hazard then, probably a toxic waste area now.

They installed a soft drink machine outside near the front door of the station. We called every cola dispenser a "Coke machine," but we mostly drank Double Cola, because it had about twice as much cola as a Coca Cola; ten ounces versus six. To a little kid, that's twice as much…to an accountant its only 67% more. We always checked the coin returns on those machines, because you never know what you might find in that dark little hole. We had heard stories about people who found a fortune in there. Once in a blue moon, you might find a nickel or a dime, or maybe the machine would give you too much change. All this was more than offset by the number of times it took your money and wouldn't give up the soft drink. Those early machines didn't bother to let you know if they were empty.

A Double Cola and a pack of peanuts or a Moon Pie was equivalent to a national holiday. I could take a big swallow, and burp to my heart's content, the louder the more satisfying. I still like doing that by the way. The best part of visiting that self-serve curb side eatery was the company of the mechanics. They didn't care how dirty we got from playing on the tires, because they were always dirtier from working on the old cars. Car engines were filthy back then. Covered from grease from their heads to their shoes, and always in a good mood, they had the same swallow-burp technique that we did, only louder. There was a full education to be had there, a lot better than that Dick and Jane stuff we were being force-fed at school. They always seemed glad to see me, and treated me better than I deserved, probably because I had two great looking older sisters, and they didn't want the little brother giving them a bad rap. You can't fault me for taking advantage of those assets. They would even let me come over and listen to the radio with them if the Yankees were playing, or in the evening if Joe Louis was fighting.

People loved Joe Louis when he was in his prime. He would defend his title almost every month, but after a long layoff during the War, he was getting a little long in the tooth for a boxing champ. He still gave every fight everything he had. He fought Jersey Joe Walcott twice during that time, and they were both great fights. Louis got knocked down in each fight, but still came back to win both of them. Those were some good memories for a first and second grader, hanging out with some gas station guys, drinking a Double Cola with some peanuts in it, and listening to Joe Louis knock out the Bum of the Month. That was about as good as life could get. There was so much hollering and excitement during those radio broadcasts, and the reception was so bad, I couldn't understand a word of what was happening among the static and the hollering. I would have to listen carefully to the men's conversation afterwards to try to figure out what actually happened. It was just being there that I liked most. Pretty soon, Mama would send Martha or Ann over to get me. They would apologize if I had been any trouble, and the guys would all stand up and say, *"Oh no, he wasn't any trouble at all."* Girls love that stuff. They would try to lead me off by the hand but I couldn't be letting those guys see me doing that.

The walk to school was about a mile. We usually hooked up with other kids who were also walking. It was kind of like riding a bus but with no bus. We did the same thing after school, but it was more of a free-for-all because everyone was giddy that school was out. The "bus" was about three blocks long, with people walking backwards and running sideways…anything to get a little extra attention.

The lady who taught my first year of school was Miss Carol Bean. She knew our whole family, and had taught almost every one of my older siblings. I remember when we got back to school after the holidays she "went around the room," as we called it, and asked each kid what they got for Christmas. Being a Willis, and everything being in alphabetical order, I was the last person to be called on. By the time the process got around to me, I had the benefit of hearing what everyone else had gotten for Christmas and I was ashamed that the cheap football I had gotten as my 'big gift' had been run over and flattened by a truck on the afternoon of Christmas day. It did make a spectacular pop, which was kind of fun, but not the kind of fun you would trade for a football. The truck driver stopped and got out of his truck, as though he had just run over our pet dog. He seemed sorry enough, but he didn't offer to buy us another football. I guess it wasn't his fault that our ball ran out in the road in front of his truck and got killed. I also received a paddle ball toy, and it lasted about an hour until we broke the rubber band. We didn't know how to fix it. We didn't know how to fix anything, really. When the only tool in your house is a hammer, every problem seems to take on the appearance of a nail. Once anything broke, it just stayed broken. A flashlight in our house became nothing more than a case for storing dead batteries. So, essentially, I was back to square one at the end of the day, and no better off than I was before Christmas had happened, and not a heck of a lot to report to my nosy teacher. If I had been mature enough, and secure enough, to tell the story just that way to the first grade class, I could have closed the show with a big laugh. Instead, I did what any red blooded, six year old, American boy would have done; I lied! I took the best of all the things I had heard from the other kids, plus a few things that I really wanted, and told the class I got all that and more. It blew the other kids away. I think I even got a round of applause.

Later, Miss Carol Bean told my mother that it sure sounded like little Buddy had a mighty fine Christmas, considering all the things that Santa had gotten him. Mama, of course, told the truth, and they both got a big chuckle out of my bodacious story. I'm pretty sure that it was a big relief to my teacher that I had made this up, since she was well aware that I was one of a handful of kids on a free lunch program at school. The poorest kids were also given free milk and graham crackers before classes got started in the morning, under the two assumptions that we weren't being fed breakfast at home and that it's hard to learn on an empty stomach. They were right about the breakfast. I don't think I had a real breakfast in the 12 years I attended the Tullahoma school system.

Those four or five kids on the free lunch program would be called out of class for a few minutes as soon as the cold milk had been delivered to the school each morning. I knew I was being singled out, and I wasn't real comfortable being in that little room for ten minutes drinking free milk and eating cookies with those poor kids. I knew the other kids back in the classroom had probably had pancakes or bacon and eggs for breakfast. I knew the teacher had "explained" us to them in euphemistic terms, without actually telling them that we didn't have two nickels to rub together. It was a little embarrassing, but still, I didn't want to give up the cookies. And that milk was real cold and right off the truck. Any milk in our home was powdered or canned, and certainly wasn't cold because we had never owned a refrigerator. Funny thing is, I didn't know any better before they started giving me milk and cookies, but after I got used to getting those things, it was hard to concentrate without them.

Neither the teacher nor Mama made me pay a price for that Christmas whopper. In fact, they found amusement in it. It meant a lot to me that they didn't dwell on my character flaw. In a strange way it made me try harder to avoid being singled out. I always thought that the fear of humiliation is a child's (if not mankind's) strongest motivator. After all, I was not the first Willis to have come through Miss Carol Bean's first grade class, and would not be the last. My older brothers and sisters before me had set a standard, and I was made aware of that fact. She managed to make the other kids know who I was, and what a "fine" family I came from. Maybe that's why she was such a darn good teacher. I tried harder and had to watch my "p's and q's" around her from then on. And although that was certainly not the last time I ever lied, whatever gene I had inherited to enable me to turn embarrassment into dogged determination was already starting to introduce itself in me. I didn't know how I was going to do it, but I was determined to get off that free lunch program.

***

Back home in the slaves' quarters, reality quickly set in. To say we didn't have two nickels was only a slight exaggeration. Everybody old enough to count money had to figure out how to earn some. Horace's job at the newspaper provided some advantages for Martha and Ann, who would sometimes work in the front office stuffing papers with circulars or whatever. The papers were five cents, so if you were going to sell papers, you had to figure out how to sell at least 20 to net fifty cents after the newspaper took half. It was a popular way for kids to make money then, and 10 year old Sara was a crackerjack.

On the nights when the newspaper was printed, Horace's bed would be empty, so 10 year old Sara slept in it until he got home. When Horace came home about daybreak, he brought home the papers for Sara to sell. As he laid the papers beside the bed for Sara, she would get up to dress as he went to bed. By sun-up she was out the door, to get a jump start with the early morning, downtown coffee drinkers.

The main coffee hangout was the Nu-Way Café. Sara was such a tenacious, early morning regular there that the owner was impressed, and took a liking to her. One day he suggested that she should leave her unsold papers there, and he would sell them for her. This was an unexpected piece of good fortune which would come to be known as a "bluebird." It was not unusual for her to get a quarter for a five cent newspaper, and on a rare occasion, 50 cents. The Tullahoma News was like butter and egg money to us, and Sara was a little cash cow. If she had been a boy, the older "paperboys" would have chased her away. But they didn't know quite what to do with a papergirl.

The Tullahoma News was sold on Wednesday and Friday. Working people liked to purchase the paper on the street rather than have a route delivery. An early bird news hustler with an honest face could figure out a way to sell 20 or 25 papers in an hour and a half before school started, if they knew where the customers were. There were no vending machines in front of the restaurants and coffee shops, so all Sara had to do was beat the other kids to the coffee shops. She had the advantage of not having to pick up the papers and she lived only a block away. She would gross a dollar or two on a good day. Again, proximity and Horace gave her a serendipitous edge, and that well earned clump of dimes in her pocket was an incredible source of self esteem for a youngster in 1948.

After school, the papers were an almost impossible sell. By that time, second hand papers were lying all over the downtown counters for the taking. So you might need a bicycle to get around and knock on a few doors. The sales pitch was pretty straightforward. Any kid that could mumble "Wanna buy a paper?" was in the club. There were basically only four responses: 1. No response, 2. "No thanks," 3. Head- shake, *no*, and 4. *"OK,"* followed by a hand in the pocket.

One Friday, Sara had 8 or 10 unsold papers left over from her morning run, and rather than turn them in to the newspaper, she had an idea. If her six year old brother, that would be me, would take the unsold papers along with her bicycle, and ride up the street for about a mile calling on each house, then come back down the other side, there could be some great opportunity for the brother. After the quick seminar, I was off.

Nothing is more exhilarating to a kid than having someone respond positively to an awkward sales pitch. Fulfilling a need and getting cash in return. Man, what a feeling!

Unfortunately, the opposite of a sale is as equally deflating. So it became a contest between the lousy feeling of rejection and the exhilaration of a sale. Suddenly, I was a salesman. Sara was depending on me after all. It was getting dark, and I knew I had to get home. I hadn't sold all the papers, but I did have a sweaty little handful of money to show for the afternoon effort. I found out later that the

Friday papers were a heck of a lot easier to sell door-to-door than the Wednesday papers were, because people are in a better mood on Friday afternoon. But I also learned that women at home were good prospects for afternoon papers. Maybe this was because her old man kept promising to bring one home, and she was in her third year of waiting.

I met Sara back at the newspaper office at dusk. She now had another nine year old girl with her, and they looked like they had been partying while I was busting my hump. They each had an ice cream cone. I could tell she was surprised that I had sold so many papers, and she wanted to see "*her*" money, which was now wet from my handling it so much. When I opened my sweaty little fist, I saw the other girl's jaw drop. She was amazed that Sara could make money while eating ice cream. Sara took the money and the two leftover papers and went inside the office to settle with the newspaper. When she returned, she handed me a dime.

Now I'm not sure what I was expecting in terms of my commission, and I knew nothing of profit margins, transportation costs or training expenses. But I felt royally screwed. A moment ago I held Fort Knox in my hand and now I felt violated. I had gone from the penthouse to the outhouse. Ten cents certainly wasn't going to get me off that free lunch program. That day, Sara had unwittingly given me my first valuable lesson in the cold, harsh realities of business, and it was an eye opener to this little man. From that day on, I knew that no matter how bad things would get for our family, there would be no reason to ever feel sorry for Sara. She would do just fine. But I would not have been nearly as disappointed if I had known then how many times in the future she would repay me.

THE MARSHALL THEATER

I'd call that bold talk for a one eyed fat man.
Robert Duvall to John Wayne in the movie True Grit, before being
shot dead on the spot.

To see a man's entire life go up in smoke over a brazen one liner like that is the stuff of legendary Western movies. We crammed our young brains full of as much of that kind of nonsense as we possibly could. Movies were our windows to the world. Sara also introduced me to the movies. The Marshall Theater was no more than a block from our house. It changed my life in so many ways. We could see the marquee from the corner as it peeked out from underneath the Pan Am sign. The highlight of the week was the Saturday matinee. I could walk by myself during the day. It usually started with at least one cartoon, and then a "serial" with the Durango Kid or Tom Mix, and ended with a good shoot-'em-up with Red Ryder or Roy Rogers. My two favorites were the Durango Kid and Lash Larue. Durango had a hideout, and a black mask, like Zorro. Lash wore guns, but his weapon of choice was a long black bullwhip. Every episode had the same plot, to which we paid no attention, because we were waiting for the ever predictable climax, where he snatched the gun out of the villain's hand with his trusty whip, chased him down on horseback, and snatched him off his horse with said same whip. Then it ended with scenes from the coming episode, which compelled us to count the days until next Saturday and the exact same plot. The heroes were just good citizens and did not get paid to do these things, but they seemed to have a knack for being in the right place at the right time when trouble started. Years later, Lash

Larue taught Harrison Ford how to do his whip tricks for those Indiana Jones movies, which also turned out to be a serial.

After the double feature, we went home and spent the rest of the afternoon re-creating the action scenes with broomstick horses and full sound effects. It took no more than two of us to form a posse, which was a favorite word, and we could head 'em off at the pass or set up an ambush. We could sneak up on crooks and get the drop on them, whatever that meant. We didn't have a whip or even a rope to make a lasso, but it didn't stop us from pretending we did. "POW-POW" was two gunshots and "ARRRGGGGG" meant that they had found their target. Just because you'd been shot a few times didn't mean you had to stop shooting back. That was only a momentary setback that showed you were a good sport, and courteous enough to give some credit to the shooting skills of your opponents. Once everybody had been killed a few dozen times, we could go on to something else, like Tarzan, for example.

Tarzan was extremely popular, and his costume was easy to mimic. Jane's outfit didn't leave a lot to the imagination either, which may explain Tarzan's popularity with young boys. We always wondered why Tarzan didn't have a beard. But before we had too much time to think about it, he would be diving out of a tree to fight an alligator. Good stuff! If you couldn't get the role of Tarzan, his chimp, Cheeta, was the next best part. Mimicking an ape was pretty easy as long as you didn't get carried away with it by bringing your monkey impersonation inside the house with you. No one really wants a monkey in the house all day and night. We would have loved to have had a Jane, but we couldn't find a decent Jane that would play with us.

Night time movies attracted a more sophisticated, adult crowd. I had to be accompanied by Sara at night. The first movie she took me to was *Bud Abbott and Lou Costello Meet Frankenstein*. It was supposed to be funny, but it scared the crap out of this seven year old. I excused myself pretending to go the restroom, and decided it was time for me to get out of there before Frankenstein came out into the audience. I neglected the small issue of telling anyone that I wasn't coming back. Sara had to leave the movie to find me. She finally found me sitting at home about three feet away from Mama, and as far as I could get from Frankenstein. This must have infuriated her, but she was so relieved to find me that all was forgiven. I still don't like scary movies and don't know why they make them.

Frankenstein was not the worst of it. The most graphic thing that ever happened in that theater was when Debra Padgett had to jump into a flaming volcano to appease the island gods. I don't remember the name of that movie, but I carried that image with me for a couple of decades. They dressed her all up with flowers in her hair, and you could see right through her sarong when she jumped. What a waste! Every boy in the theater was in love with her. That just about did me in. I have since learned to tell the difference between reality and the magic of the movies; but, just like Santa, the movies were a lot more fun before I made that discovery. Movies have a powerful influence on children and I hope the people who make them are sensitive to that.

***

Sometime after the holidays, the Willis family plight had been widely circulated, assimilated and verified throughout our small town. As it turned out, being close to the synergy of town had some benefits. People got to know us, and there was plenty of friendly conversation in town. The proximity and the convenience of stores and shops provided opportunity. Martha was approached by a downtown department store owner to work as a clerk to attract her high school peers to do business there. This turned out to be a good strategy for the owner of Davis's, as Martha was one of the most beautiful and popular girls to ever *"set foot"* inside Tullahoma High School. That is exactly the way Mama would have expressed that, split infinitive and all.

Setting up lemonade stands, selling newspapers, raking leaves, mowing lawns and babysitting were about the only respectable ways to make money for anyone under sixteen. In order to have a real job, kids under 16 needed a work permit. This meant parental consent, restricted hours, supervision requirements and a bunch of scary, red tape stuff. This was a way of protecting children so they could stay home and cut a couple of acres of weeds with a sharp sling blade.

Ann was only 15 years old when Martha was invited to work at Davis', and, therefore, not yet eligible to work without a special permit. As soon as she turned 16, she was invited to join her sister Martha as a sales clerk. Their youth and enthusiasm was a welcome breath of fresh air for the older customers. The girls loved to show off all the new fashions and enjoyed their unlikely role as "fashion consultants." It didn't hurt that they were both very beautiful teenagers. They spread the word with their girlfriends at school when there was a special sale, and the store management was delighted, but they were never properly compensated. Most of their pay was in the form of discounted clothing.

Mama had always demanded that her children were "presentable" when they left the house. So, out of necessity, Mama had to teach herself to sew. Making clothes was cheaper than buying clothes, so she became an expert seamstress. She was always hemming trousers, replacing buttons and altering hand-me-downs. She couldn't afford to throw away a perfectly good sock just because it had a hole in it. She had a Singer sewing machine with a foot peddle. With a child in practically every grade at school, special events and school plays came around more often than the electric bill. Mama could dye a pair of long handle underwear, and make a pair of pointy shoes, and turn you into Robin Hood before Errol Flynn could get out of the sack. And, trust me; any boy who surprises his teacher with a pair of green tights is indeed, "*in like Flynn.*" I always got a good role in the school play, but in my green tights I even got a singing part.

"*In Sherwood Forrest, the merriest of lives is our outlaw's life so free. We roam and rove in Sherwood's leafy grove underneath the tall greenwood tree.*" I know the rest but I don't want to bore you with a first grade play.

It was a common practice to make girls' dresses from paper cutout patterns purchased from a department store. From the time her girls were 10 or 12, Mother had made their school clothes from patterns the girls had chosen for themselves at Wilson's Department Store. It was a natural transition for this clever seamstress to earn a little money doing alterations and custom sewing for others. Over the years, Mother sewed for many of Tullahoma's most prominent citizens. Martha and Ann were two of her walking advertisements.

***

Horace lived a vampire's life at the newspaper working late hours and sleeping during the day. On nights that he didn't work he led an active social life of his own, his only reward for the sacrifices he made in giving up the rest of his life. I was too young to appreciate the sacrifices he was making. I just thought he was lucky that he didn't have homework.

Martha was old enough to be dating now. Horace had a friend named George Thrower, who had a car, and he would stop by the house from time to time. They played football together on the same B Team at high school, and as friends, George was very familiar with Horace's situation at home and at work. George was also trying to get better acquainted with Martha, and did not realize she was Horace's sister when he first met her. He was a couple of years older than Martha. Martha still had a year or so of high school to complete when they met. George, who was an only child, seemed to tolerate of all the chaos that constantly surrounded our house, and even seemed to be entertained by it. He was friendly and interested in every one of Martha's eight siblings, and this impressed Mama, who liked him immediately. We had no idea at the time what an important contribution that George would make in our lives.

As exciting as downtown was for us, living there must have been a rough couple of years for Mama. Watching her kids walk long distances to and from school, sometimes in the pouring rain, and trying to make ends meet with little or no income, was no fun for her. After school, everyone who was old enough to count money would work to try to earn a little. Ann, at 15, had a work permit to work at the Tullahoma News. There was always a need for odd jobs like sorting papers or putting circulars in them. Most of these activities took place near the front office where businessmen came and went. In those days, every workplace was a hostile environment for a pretty girl, and Ann was beginning to fill out her handmade clothes very nicely. Neither she nor her mother was very pleased with some of the remarks thrown her way by some of the businessmen who stopped by. It was commonplace in those days for grown men to flirt with young girls, and nothing was done to check the behavior. These men were clients, after all, and there was no such thing as sexual harassment or a human resources department. In those days, all women, regardless of age, endured annoying behavior wherever they went.

On weekends, the little ones were having a field day hanging out at the movies and their favorite hangouts. Tommy did odd jobs in the pool hall, and would come home late, smelling like cigarette smoke. Mama was having trouble keeping up with all these comings and goings. Her mother's intuition was telling her that living downtown was not a healthy situation, and needed to be as temporary as possible.

There is a tide in the affairs of men.
Which, taken at the flood, leads on to fortune:
Omitted, all the voyage of their life
Is bound in shallows and in miseries.
William Shakespeare
Brutus, Julius Caesar, Act 4.

I believe that there are ordinary people on this earth who possess a second, deeper intellect: an innate ability to anticipate the future and to steel their resolve and moral obligation to their duty. This is a contract that is born into them, and they are instinctively driven to action. These actions almost always produce desirable results. Why this sense of moral obligation is crystal clear only to certain people when the same logic is available to everyone all around them is unexplainable. They know what they have to do, and they do it without blinking. They never have to be reduced to saying, "Well, that didn't occur to me" because it did occur to them, and moreover, they behaved accordingly. Cicero used a similar analogy in his writing about the people who shaped the Roman Empire. In my lifetime, I have had the privilege of knowing a few of these people, and I have tried my best to become a member of that small society.

My first exposure to this behavior was the night that my oldest brother took the initiative to lift his family out of the pit of tyranny that represented our lives to that point, to clear the way for Mama and her children to chart their own destiny. For good or evil, these people provide the dynamics that change our lives. Even though she had no map, my mother's true Bluestocking spirit rose to the occasion, and she began her own courageous journey that not only guided us through some difficult times, but eventually amazed and delighted her nine bewildered kids. Her practical, country wisdom kept us safe, and her unique style of situational management allowed each one of us to develop our individual strengths and personalities. She was determined not to allow our minds to be diluted with mediocrity. Like the pigeons that graze on the concrete slabs of Time Square, she got us up every day and kept our feet moving. She knew we were not allowed to miss a day of pecking, because it was in that activity that something good might happen. Inactivity was death, and not acceptable. By her example, she transferred that same resolve to duty that became her mantra. These simple stories give testimony to her and to mothers like her, who have the uncanny ability to will good things to happen by pressing on, no matter what.

Turning Points

In the summer of '49, as soon as school was out, Mama executed her escape from downtown. She had shared her plan with a friend in the grocery community and with some of her "estranged" husband's employers. Everyone was more than glad to help Mama if they could. Warren Angel, who owned a grocery store downtown, had a vacant house across the street from East Lincoln Elementary School, which was about two blocks from the high school. This location would solve several school transportation problems, and remove the temptations of urban life, which were her two main priorities.

One of the mechanics at the filling station had a truck, and she hired him and two of his buddies to help move some of our things. They even brought watermelons. We all pitched in to help move, and it was an exciting weekend. After the move, we all gathered in the backyard and ate those cold watermelons. To our surprise, some neighborhood kids came over to see what was going on, and got in on the watermelon feast. This was indeed going to be a different situation, and an interesting one.

Necessity has always been the mother of invention. We'd lost some opportunities by moving away from downtown so we had to pick up some new ones. Everybody had to ramp up and get creative. By now, Mama's reputation as a seamstress had spread. Plaids and pleats were all the fashion and not easy to put together perfectly. Even the expensive "store-bought" pleats and plaid dresses had their imperfections. For some reason, this was fairly easy for Mama, and people seemed to know she was pretty good at building dresses from the ground up. She made custom prom gowns and party dresses, but also took in alterations.

Prom season was my absolute favorite time of the year, although I didn't even know what a prom was. Mama made prom dresses. It took several fittings to get a prom dress just right. These serial fittings usually took place right after school and in our living room. This was a huge part of my overall education. I discovered all this enlightenment completely by accident by walking in from school one afternoon and there was 17 year old Elaine Kaplan, being pinned around the waist with nothing on from there up. No bra, no nothing! I was only in the third grade, and she just said... "Hi!" Mama had a mouthful of pins and couldn't say anything. I was in total shock, and just stood there staring like a love struck idiot. I can still see it all in my mind's eye. I think the dress was white, but everything else was pink and perfect. She would have made the ideal Jane (for our Tarzan escapades). Even though I had seen my sisters traipsing around the house in their underwear many times, this was entirely different, and confusing. It was a feeling that I knew I would have to sort out entirely on my own, in complete privacy.

A week or so later, I was on the front porch when Elaine Kaplan came by for another fitting, and she gave me a wink. You can't buy excitement like that. I don't know if that qualifies her as my first girlfriend, but I was definitely in love. Until then, I had never paid attention to the structural integrity of that old house or to privacy issues caused by old doors that wouldn't completely shut, but that was the day I discovered a huge, wonderful crack in the dressing room door. I would later find myself going two or three blocks out of the way just to walk past the Kaplan house, hoping to find Elaine out in the yard, naked.

The older sisters would work in the department store on weekends and during special sales events. Once again, we all had to figure out some way to put some jingle in our pockets or do without. I might have been left totally out of cash opportunities except for that wonderful time-saving invention called the bicycle. Here again, Horace brought home the newspapers, and Sara and I would peddle them. Thank God for the Tullahoma News.

I first tried to sell my papers downtown, but the place was saturated with newspapers. I didn't know whether to stay in one place or peddle around. I learned quickly that it was easier to say no to a kid on a bicycle than one who is standing in front of you extending a fresh newspaper. Someone suggested that I try the Genesco Shoe Factory where everyone went into work around 7 am, and it worked.

Finally, I had found a niche, until a skinny little kid with an asthmatic condition, whose daddy dropped him off in a car, starting horning into my territory. He was getting a lot of sympathy sales. It took me a long time to be friends with him, but one day it was raining real hard, and his daddy asked if I wanted a ride home. I told him I had a bike, and he got out of his car and into the pouring rain and made room for it in the trunk. After he took me home, he got back out of his warm car and into the downpour again to get the bike out for me. I couldn't hate them any more after that.

In the evenings, especially on weekends, both Martha and Ann were in demand as babysitters. It didn't pay much, but it provided a quiet place to do homework and a welcome break from the chaos at home.

The Willis girls were good, cheap labor. Being available and willing opened the door, but being able kept them in demand. If the only appliance in your house is a cooking stove, being invited to baby sit a couple of kids in a fine home with a TV and a fridge full of snacks is a luxury ride for a teenager. When the parents got home from their night out and found their house better off than when they left it, and their kids sleeping peacefully, fifty cents an hour seemed like an excellent investment to them. The hardest part of that job had to be the ride home with Mr. Big. All juiced up from his night on the town, and feeling good and sassy, he's now driving the young babysitter home. *"You can sit up here with me if you like,"* has got to be a babysitter's worst nightmare.

It took only a few days at 719 East Lincoln Street to realize that Warren Angel's rental house was far from vacant. In addition to being dilapidated with wood rot and termites, the crawl space was like a wildlife reserve. Rabbits, raccoons, possums, skunks, feral cats, stray dogs, and any kind of pregnant four legged animal would seek refuge under that house as their maternity ward. We dared not board it up for fear of what we might be trapping under there. Mama was unfazed by all this, and told us we should learn to live in harmony with nature, her way of making the best of a bad situation.

The inside of the house was infested with cockroaches and mice. They must have thought we were trying to starve them out, because we weren't much of a food source for them. I'm not even certain that we were on the top of the food chain there. We didn't know that the asbestos shingles on that house were harmful, or lead based paint, or that playing with mercury from a broken thermometer was poisonous. But none of it killed us. There was a huge oak tree in the front yard and the heavy limbs hung perilously close to the house. We all wondered what might happen if one of those limbs, or God forbid, the entire tree, were to fall on that rickety tin roof. There was no insulation between the metal on the roof and the ceilings to the rooms upstairs. In the wintertime we used the coats we wore to school for extra cover on the bed. If you put a glass of water beside the bed, it might be solid ice when you woke up the next morning.

All who could work worked, and we didn't starve. We lived within 100 yards of a grocery store owned by Monroe York. None of us ever worked at York's, but we did scavenge soft drink bottles that he would pay us to return, for a penny each. He stored the bottles behind the store for a long time, in clear view of anyone walking down the back alley. He was a very good businessman but that was not the smartest thing he ever did.

His radio commercials gave a whole new meaning to ad nauseam. Day and night, the radio blared, "*York's, York's, York's!*" But it must have worked. His grocery business was brisk. We heard a joke on the owner that someone had accused him of running a clever scam as a check out gimmick. The story was that he kept a store item, like a broom, permanently stationed at the end of the checkout counter. This item was added to everybody's bill, but the item never went home with anybody. In those days there was no such thing as an itemized computer printout. If the customer questioned the bill, Monroe could make it appear like an innocent mistake by pointing to the planted item, "*Oh! This is not your broom?*" What made the joke funnier is the fact that he did keep a broom there, never mind that it was (probably) for sweeping the front of the store.

Before there were lotteries, there were drawings for Thanksgiving turkeys and Christmas hams. York's had a free drawing for a Thanksgiving turkey every year, and, with discretion, we could register as many times as we wanted. We would duck out of sight around the corner of the aisle and fill out dozens of entries each. In several years of doing this and hundreds of entries, we only won one turkey.

Sometimes, the store had introductory free samples of new products. We are the reason that most stores would later add the caveat, "one per customer." When they introduced Golden Crisp cereal in 1949, they gave it away in large cellophane bags that held a cubic foot of cereal, and the puffed up stuff weighed practically nothing. We cleaned the store out. We ate them right out of the sack. Mama found those little puffed wheat nuggets stuck to just about everything in that house for the better part of a year. Of course, after the promotion was over, we never bought a single box of Golden Crisps.

We lived next door to the Hardaways. Mrs. Hardaway was our landlord's sister. Her husband, Herbert, ran one of Mr. Angel's grocery stores downtown. They competed with York's by offering to deliver groceries for free. They had a red pickup truck for that purpose, which they kept parked in front of their house. The truck advertised their free delivery service on both sides and on the tailgate. It seemed odd to me that it would have been misspelled it in all three places, but there it was… Free Deliver! I guess they were happy with it, because it never changed. We hitched many a ride to town in the back of that pickup.

EAST LINCOLN STREET

*One aspect of serendipity is that you have to be looking
for something to find something else.*
>   Lawrence Block

That run-down, story-and-a-half house with the broken asbestos
shingles would become ground-zero for every bored kid within ped-
dling distance. No matter what age they happened to be, the nine
Willis's had someone to match up with them. Our house was the
local playground. This is where I learned to whistle seven different
ways, ride a bike backwards, shoot a jump shot and play 52-Card
Pickup. The neighborhood had more wide open spaces for baseball,
football games, marbles, hide and seek, kick the can, mumble-peg
and Annie Over.

On warm summer nights, that little concrete-slab porch with the
aluminum glider could turn into a Shakespearean fantasyland. With
the smell of the wild honeysuckle that had smothered the overgrown
bushes in the side yard, and the teasing of lightening bugs beckoning
like pixie fairies, *"Why are you sitting on the porch?"* Some nights, it
was hard to go to bed. Mama didn't really impose a strict bedtime
for any of us. We were just expected to have common sense.

The schools were across the street with basketball goals, football
fields and a baseball diamond…and the city actually mowed the
grass. All this suited Mama much better than downtown. She could
keep tabs on us, and it was a healthier environment for kids. But she
had her sights set on a grander plan. Her focus was on preparing for
the first of many milestones, the graduation of her oldest daughter.

Martha was a 17 year old high school senior (and Ann was close behind).

Laziness is poverty's biggest challenge. You have to fight it every day, or it will set in like rigor mortis. But if you keep your feet moving and the energy flowing, you can give serendipity a chance to make something happen. There is one thing for certain: nothing good comes from doing nothing. We were not always going in any specific direction, but we were going, usually in just about every direction. When we didn't have anything else, we had this basic principle going for us. Occasionally, something good did happen.

In 1950, Martha was voted the most beautiful girl in her senior class. She was asked to represent the school that year in the Miss Tullahoma Beauty Pageant. This would have been quite an honor in an ordinary household, but Mama was worried sick over her oldest daughter's first spotlight performance. The fact that her competition would not be wearing 'home made' gowns was not lost our matriarch. They could have thrown in the towel right then and there. But it didn't seem to bother Martha, who had a bold, secret plan to capture her own red carpet showstopper.

Martha took Ann with her one afternoon after school to call on Mrs. Frances Harton. The John Hartons were probably the wealthiest people in town, if not in the entire state of Tennessee at that time. The girls knew that the Hartons had three grown daughters of their own, and that there were all kinds of fancy dresses somewhere in that big house. The plan was to get their hands on one of them. When Mrs. Harton came to the door, Martha simply explained her situation. Then she just flat out asked if she could borrow one of her girls' dresses for the beauty contest. Just like that. As surprised as Mrs. Harton must have been at that point-blank proposal, she explained that all those things were tucked away in the attic, and, since her maid was not there that day, she was not sure she could climb all the way up in the attic to get them. In other words, go away! Unfazed, Martha pressed on. *"If you would be kind enough to show us where they are, perhaps we could climb up there to look at them."* Having daughters of her own, and realizing she was no match for a determined teenager on a mission, the wonderful lady completely caved in, and swung her front door open to them. Not only did she climb up there with the girls where boxes and boxes of beautiful things were stored, but she selected three particularly special chests, flung the tops open and instructed the girls to help themselves. The two young Cinderellas were left alone for several hours to shop at will.

The final choice was indeed a winner. Three weeks later Martha stood alone on stage in front of a standing room only crowd at the Marshall Theater with flashbulbs blazing off her crown. The rambunctious crowd had been pulling for her all evening, and when the winner was finally announced, the Tullahoma News reported the "thunderous ovation." She was an overnight celebrity. Our sister was Miss Tullahoma. Whatever else that dress had ever been involved in, it had never seen a more exciting night than that.

Martha had to leave for Nashville Business College immediately, so she didn't compete in the regional beauty contest in Murfreesboro. But she didn't care. It wouldn't have topped that. We didn't have time to sit around on our laurels anyway. We still didn't have a refrigerator. But she had set the bar pretty high, and her mother wasted no time pointing that out to the rest of us.

While all this drama was being played out, our sister Ann was also busy ruining the curve for the rest of us. Ann was president of her class and just about every other club she joined. She was an honor student, a basketball star, the head majorette, and the Editor in Chief of her yearbook. She was an achieving, blond ball of positive energy, full of determination and spunk. She was also very beautiful and a natural born leader.

ANN

Its beauty that captures your attention,
Personality that captures your heart.
 Unknown

If my mother ever came close to getting it just right, it would have been with Ann. She was the youngest of Mama's three Depression era children and the enormous wake that Ann left behind at Tullahoma High made it easier in many ways for the next three to draft behind her. Ann was the epitome of what a role model should be, and her teachers loved her. More than a beautiful girl with a magnetic personality, she was a natural and competent leader. Open and honest, she was trustworthy to the core and faithful to her friends and to her beliefs. If Ann loved you, she loved you warts and all and she loved you forever. She was the kind of sister that every young boy would like to have, but she sure set the academic bar real high. Her younger brother Tommy had plenty of momentum going for him following the trail that she had blazed.

When Ann was a senior in high school, in 1951, she also represented her class in the Miss Tullahoma beauty contest. Since it had worked before, Ann thought about going back to the Harton attic, but this time Mama got into the act, determined to create a dress for Ann just as glamorous as the Harton gown. This took many fittings and a lot of co-operation between fittee and fitter, and they worked on the masterpiece until the eleventh hour. There was not even time to hem the dress before the evening of the contest, so they decided to chop it off at the proper length and forget about the hem. Mama said those male judges wouldn't be looking at Ann's hem anyway.

"Lo and Behold!" was one of Mama's favorite expressions when something good ever happened to one of us, and we got to hear it again that night, because after Ann won that crown, kudos and accolades rained down on the Willis household like a ticker tape parade. Even the animals living under our house were having a party. Never before had two sisters won that title back-to-back, and I'm pretty sure that it hasn't happened since. For one thing, most families don't have children one year apart, much less two bombshells. The whole town was thrilled for us.

Mama taught us not to get too excited, and full of ourselves, whenever something good happened to us; and, likewise, not to get too down on ourselves if it didn't. *"These things are just part of life."* But even she was dumbfounded and half frightened by all the attention. After all that she'd been through, she was not one for displaying a lot of emotion, but she couldn't help having a little cry over it. There was no way for me to know how much work the girls had put into all that. What did I know? I still had to peddle newspapers, and whatever they did didn't affect my standard of living. We still didn't have what most people would call the basic essentials. Like food, for example.

Ann graduated high school in May of 1951. She left almost immediately for the "Athens of the South" (Nashville) for X-ray technology studies at Vanderbilt University. Even Mama knew that Madame Marie Curie had died of radiation induced cancer from fooling with that stuff, but that didn't stop Ann. Radiology was a key part of all the new technology that our scientists were throwing at us and the radiology industry was coming on strong. The concept of looking at pictures of the inside of the body was not new, but modern radiology had new medical implications, and enormous economic potential.

Ann's X-ray schooling was one of those "sing for your supper" programs where you didn't have to pay for the school, but you had to work at the hospital to earn it. This was a hard and scary time for her. The hours were long and food was not included. She basically lived on apples, and peanut butter and crackers.

She had been dating James E. Martin, a Tullahoma High upper grad who had distinguished himself as a very fine baseball player with the pro scouts. His baseball moniker was "Boog" (athletes like to give each other weird nicknames). He was also the son of Buddy Martin, a small craft airplane pilot and aviation promoter. Later in life, he also preferred the nickname "Buddy." Ann was nuts about this Martin guy, who had a great motorcycle with an Indian on it. Ann would sometimes take weekend rides on the back of it with him, and it drove Mama nuts. When he brought the shiny bike by the house, he was swarmed by a bunch of dirty kids, who all wanted to touch it and sit on it. That drove him nuts. He had to stand out there and guard his bike while he waited on Ann. He was an only child, and wasn't used to all that chaos. That bike was like honey to a swarm of flies, and he didn't bring a fly swatter. He only made the mistake of bringing that bike around our neighborhood a couple of times.

Mama was somewhat of a blurter. If she was thinking something she just might say it out loud, even though it might be totally inappropriate. The first time she was introduced to Buddy, her first words to him were. "*Well! You're not nearly as good looking as your Daddy.*" But he was plenty good looking for Ann. Buddy tried to make it in the "bigs" (Major League Baseball) by way of a farm team in the Florida State League. His stats were great, but when he tore the muscle in the shoulder of his throwing arm, the journey came to an abrupt end. No more fun and games! The U.S. Air Force and the real world were waiting for him.

In 1952, Martha married George Robert Thrower, mechanical engineer and her long time boyfriend. Mama loved George; he adored Martha, was Horace's pal, and was extremely tolerant if not entertained by all the family chaos, which was constant. He also bragged on Mama's cooking. George worked at the Army Ballistic Missile Command at Redstone Arsenal in Huntsville, Alabama, about 60 miles from Tullahoma.

Since Martha was a government employee, it was not difficult for her to receive the necessary references for a new job and a transfer from AEDC to another government job. Martha joined her new husband in Huntsville and worked, conveniently, as a secretary for the Army Rocket and Guided Missile Research and Development Division in their legal department.

Hank Williams

When I was ten years old in 1952 I could sing every one of Hank Williams songs, and did, just about every day. The broom was my guitar and I was pretty darn good. *"Long Gone Lonesome Blues"* was my favorite, and I often got requests for that one. Ann was going to school in Nashville, and she surprised us that summer by inviting me and my eight year old brother Tykie to come to the Grand Ole Opry. Hank was on the program to perform around 10 pm Saturday night. When six year old Jimmy (Beau) heard about this, he went bonkers and we couldn't resist bringing him along. Ann hosted us for the weekend and had a full agenda for us. We were getting the redneck-red-carpet treatment, and were pumped up for a once in a lifetime opportunity to see Hank. She presented us with a Slinky, which we played with on the stairs of her apartment until we left for the Ryman Auditorium. If you don't remember the Slinky, it was a fairly useless object but very entertaining when pushed down a flight of steps. (That could also describe some of the people I have worked with over the years.)

Ten o'clock came and went and no Hank. With each new performer we thought surely Hank would come on stage next, because it was getting late. Tykie and Beau hit a wall at 11:30, and were sound asleep, and I was hanging on with one eye open. Finally, at midnight, they announced that they were sorry, but it looked like Hank wasn't going to make it, so he was an official *"No Show."* Poor Ann was stuck with three worn out kids that had to be moved across town at midnight. Hank lost some of his luster with me that night. Little did I know that Hank didn't have that many performances left in him. He was apparently trying to live out the lyrics he wrote. Like one of his songs says, *"No matter how I struggle and strive, I'll never get out of this world alive."*

One of Ann's job assignments at the Vanderbilt hospital was to work a rotating shift on the admissions desk. Late one Saturday night, a few weeks after our Opry episode, she finally saw Hank when his wife Audrey brought him in to be admitted for treatment. He was so heavily under the influence (of something) that he could neither speak nor control his motor senses. Ann was nervous taking the admissions information from Audrey, because she felt that Audrey was just making up some of the answers that she didn't know, and Ann wasn't sure how serious this situation might be. She didn't want Hank Williams to croak on her watch.

Hank didn't croak that night, and both he and Ann managed to live through that hospital visit. But Hank didn't last much longer. Apparently, he put the bottle to his head and pulled the trigger. On New Year's Eve of that same year, he was pronounced dead. He died in the back seat of his car with his driver in the front seat on the way to a New Year's Eve performance. It was a long, bitterly cold road trip, and Hank was wrapped in a blanket after being heavily sedated from "not feeling well." He had been dead for almost a day before his driver even knew it. On the first day of 1953, the radio brought us the sad news. They said he was found dead in his car but they gave no details. He was only 29 years old, but he had been reckless with alcohol and pills for several years, including the night Ann went to all that trouble for her three little brothers. She probably could have used a couple of Hank's pills that night herself.

After Ann finished her work at Vanderbilt in 1955, she married Buddy Martin at the United Methodist Church in Tullahoma. I was 14. We found their get-a-way car and tied cans and old shoes behind it, and marked it up with white shoe polish. I tried to write "Just Married" on the side window and somehow misspelled it to read "Just Marred." You can't white-out white shoe polish, so I tried to use the "burnt toast" excuse that I did it on purpose, but I think they all knew I screwed up their art work. The newlyweds moved to Columbus, Ohio, where Buddy was stationed at the Air Force Strategic Air Command Base, and Ann took a job at Dennison Engineering Company. That was the first of many moves for them.

Today Show Green Room

New York City
Thursday, November 13, 2008, 8:45am

Lee and I waited for 10 minutes in the lobby of the Club Quarters Hotel to be escorted to the Green Room at the NBC news building two blocks away. It was a humid, overcast day in New York. Lee asked our escort, David, if he was there to protect us from the camels when we walked past them. David seemed not to notice them, as though his job was a daily three ring circus with NBC.

The rain that had been forecast would not begin until later in the afternoon. Thirty or forty people milled around in the waiting area and some of them recognized us from pictures that had been used to promote the seventh episode of *"Everyone Has a Story."* Kathie Lee Gifford came in with her hair up in four inch curlers, and rushed over to me immediately. They had been highly anticipating this show and had been running pictures of me all week. I looked at her hair and asked if she was transmitting or receiving with all that equipment on her head. She got it immediately and said *"Both, I hope."* After I introduced her to Lee, who was by far the best looking woman in the room, Kathie Lee apologized for the curlers. I told her that the only time that I had ever seen a woman in curlers that big, there had been a tornado in a trailer park somewhere. She laughed from the gut, just like we had known each other for 20 years.

I talked to Aaron Lazar and David Friedman most of the hour. Freidman was pecking on his laptop just as I am doing at this very moment. He was working on another song. He had helped write a song for my story, and Aaron was to sing it on the air. It was supposed to be a surprise to me for some reason, so I had never heard it. Aaron had just starred in *Tale of Two Cities* on Broadway which had closed that very week. I asked him about his next project, and he said there might be something pretty exciting if Andrew Lloyd Weber completed his plans for a sequel to *Phantom of The Opera*. Weber had suggested to Aaron that he was up for the lead, and the title might be *Love and Dying*. This all came with a huge disclaimer, as there are no certainties in the entertainment business, especially on Broadway in an economy that we were likely to be facing after this financial meltdown.

As the songwriter and piano player, David Friedman sat on the sofa with his laptop open, several celebrities making TV appearances that morning sat in the makeup chairs in front of the mirrors being combed and dusted. One of the comedians on *30 Rock* was one of them. The only person he made eye contact with was himself when he looked in the mirror. It has always puzzled me why some people are humble before they achieve success and become smug and indifferent afterward. His own mother would have jerked a knot in his tail if she could have seen how foolish he looked trying to be a big shot. There was a great opportunity to spend two or three minutes spreading a little comedic sunshine around that room, but he wasted it. Later, on camera, the comedian was trying to turn on the charm with Kathie Lee and Hoda but he had already blown it with me. I wasn't feeling the love from Mr. Tracy Morgan.

Freidman was just the opposite, interrupting his writing to chat with us about his work and to introduce Lee and me to Dave Bellochio, the keyboard player. Dave is a very personable guy who is really a rocker, and he had long hair almost down to his shoulders. Most of the songs I'd heard that were written for this TODAY show series were sappy little Broadway type ballads, and I imagined that some of his rocker dudes were probably jabbing him for landing the job as Kathie Lee's keyboard musician. He was waiting to go through hair and makeup, and he said they usually changed his hair for the show. I pointed to what was left of mine and told him to enjoy his hair while he could. He was only about 30 and I could see that he was already thinning a little on top. He had brought a whole table of puff pastries for the crew. What a nice guy! All these artists were so relaxed and confident. I was hoping that all of them were making a fortune doing what they were doing, but when you are living in New York City, whatever your paycheck is, it's not enough. Give me good, hard working people over celebrities any day.

Jayme came out and sat with us and got to know Lee. She had everything planned out in her head, and told me what they were likely to ask me on the show, but I don't remember a thing she said. I got a bottle of water and just tried to keep my throat from locking up.

Part II - The Fifties Era

The Happy Days

A popular television show would later depict the Fifties as the "Happy Days," and speaking for myself, I could not agree more. But underneath all the teeny bopping rock and roll and 'ramma lamma ding dong,' there was a strange, Cold War atmosphere of national paranoia. Communism, nuclear bombs, and superpower posturing clouded the entire culture. That decade had its own unique set of psychological challenges. Richie Cunningham's TV show did not focus on the weekly civil defense drills at school, or the nation's obsession with fallout shelters, but every parent and teacher in America did, and it scared the devil out of everybody.

Ozzie and Harriet Nelson seemed normal enough on TV but look how trashy little Ricky turned out. James Dean, Marilyn Monroe, and Elvis Presley were also products of this period, if that tells you anything. The Fifties was an odd time of individual behavior and personal discovery. Somewhere between Buddy Holley, The Big Bopper and the military draft, it was the perfect storm for confused teenagers.

McCarthyism had created an atmosphere that tended to foster an every-man-for-himself attitude. Overlaying all this, the dreaded military draft hung over the heads of teenage boys like an anvil. If you were healthy, and your family didn't have enough political clout to avoid it, military service was not a choice, it was a requirement, and young men had to deal with it one way or another. At a certain age we were required to register for the draft. We could either join one of the branches of military service or wait until our number came up, and it would come up. My role model older brother would soon be registering for the draft and I wasn't very far behind.

Tommy was the oldest of the three middle children, followed by Sara and myself. For the purposes of this book anyway, we represented the Fifties generation. Being caught in the middle, as we were, is supposed to be a double-edged sword, and I was never sure what it meant to be a middle child. Several books have been written about the birth order of siblings and their behavior. I never understood that kind of nonsense. As far as I could tell, life was a single roll of the dice, and no matter how many sevens or snake-eyes had been rolled before me, when my turn came around, I had the same odds on my roll of the dice as anybody else. A basic law of statistics! The fact that I was a "middle child" and was sandwiched between three Depression-era children and three Baby Boomers never occurred to me as being good or bad. As far as I was concerned, I was still just Number Six. Give me the dice.

Growing Up On A Shoestring

Food is the rock on which we build. Oscar Wilde

In the early 1950's, food assistance was available for needy people who were eligible and who signed up for it. Three items in particular were regularly distributed to all who qualified: flour, cheese and oleo. Oleo means oil, but this was a butter substitute. Most people called it margarine. It was a white, and in the shape of a brick. You had to mix it with an orange power to make it turn yellow (like that was the magic that somehow turned it into real butter). Most people think butter is yellow because it already has the food coloring in it. Perception is reality.

We could have used all of that free stuff, but there was not a chance in a million that my mother would have signed up or stood in the line for the hand out. We went along with that of course, just like we went along with a lot of things that parents did that made no sense; like when they told us not to put beans in our ears, or that if you cross your eyes, they will get stuck that way. This kind of information only makes you want to go find some beans and cross your eyes immediately. But not accepting those handouts was her way of telling us that we needed to *"stand on our own two feet."*

Our little brains were like blank sheets of paper, being filled in every day by Mama and our elementary school teachers. The old *tabula rasa* theory! They did give us very useful information such as the four basic food groups. When Tykie came home from school and told Mother that his teacher said we were supposed to be eating fruit every day, she had a simple response. *"The teacher didn't happen to give you any did she?"* He knew that meant he wasn't going to be enjoying one of the four basic food groups that day. The good news is that we weren't always snacking on sugary treats, like cookies and candy. We did have cake at least nine times a year because Mother always made a cake if someone had a birthday. As for the rest of the year, if you asked for a cookie you always got one of two famous replies, *"I'll make you think cookie!"* or the parental classic, *"You'll think cookie when I'm through with you!"* In other words, there were no cookies, so quit whining. These were not offered as threats; they were just automatic comments that came out as though you had just pulled a string on a 1950's Mama-doll.

The problem with food is that once you've gotten accustomed to it, you tend to develop an addiction to it. It's not so hard to skip a meal, but it's hard to skip a whole day. The good news is that when you are hungry, you are not all that picky, and you will take your carbohydrates any way you can get them. Trying to feed a houseful of kids day after day with no folding money is like grazing cattle on a flat rock, but Mama could make a meal out of a saltine cracker. Spread on a little miracle butter (oleo), some sugar and cinnamon, and it's out the door with you. It's better if it's toasted, but who can wait for that? Her fast food kitchen was run on a shoestring budget. Absolutely nothing was wasted, not even the fat from a frying pan. There was no such thing as an expiration date, because anything we opened we never even had to put the top back on.

We purchased our groceries on Friday evening, when someone had a paycheck to be cashed. Mama could make $10 into meals for all of us for the entire weekend. Her meals were inspired by the lowest cost canned or seasonal ingredients. It all started with a 10 pound sack of Idaho potatoes. Pinto beans, powdered milk, bread and canned tomatoes were staple items. A whole chicken was cheaper that cut up chicken. Hamburger helper had not been invented, but she had her own ground beef stretcher; bread or corn meal. Anything that was edible right out of the paper bag was in danger of being consumed on the spot, so she had to protect those items. Picture a bird feeding her chicks and you've just about got it. And I would have to say, that this was one of her greatest achievements. Where most people would look into an empty pantry and see nothing but a half bag of rice, a few raisins and some corn meal, Mama pictured rice pudding and hot corn cakes. Borrowing a cup of something from a neighbor was always a viable option. After all, our next door neighbor ran a grocery store.

In the wintertime, Mama would stew tomatoes in powdered milk with a pat of margarine. With a little salt and pepper and a couple of saltine crackers, that little bowl of tomato soup was enough to get us ready to build a snowball fort. For dinner, a hot bowl of pinto beans with chopped onions, Cole slaw and corn bread was gourmet heaven, and not unhealthy. She made sure we had a garden in the summer, something she knew how to do from her youth. Even though she had plenty of "man power" she seemed to do most of the work herself, not because it was work, but because she enjoyed it. Corn and tomatoes, maybe some okra, squash, green onions, and field peas are about all I can remember coming out of that little plot in all the years we kept our little victory garden. When the tomatoes got ripe in early July she made BLT sandwiches without the B or the L. We ate tomatoes right off the vine with a salt shaker. We had sliced tomatoes, tomato soup, fried green tomatoes, and tomatoes and macaroni. She would can some of the tomatoes, presumably for storage, but for some reason, they always got eaten within a few days. I always helped out with the canning process because I liked fooling around in the kitchen and I was curious about cooking. That's when I learned something about people who *can* food. Long after they have quit canning, they continue to hoard Mason jars, and simply cannot bring themselves to throw one away.

I don't mean to make it sound like we were the only people in America living this way, but few lived with less, and Mother was an expert in making it seem like we were just a normal family. Complaining and whining was simply not allowed. As far as she was concerned, we were doing just fine. As long as she kept adults out of our ramshackled house, so they couldn't see the chaos and clutter, she could continue to perpetuate an illusion of normality. She could only do so much, and she didn't like constantly nagging her kids about keeping the house straight. She also didn't encourage having pets around the house, for obvious reasons. She didn't need anything else to feed, step over, clean up after, or care for when it got sick.

Mama hated for anyone to think that her kids were inferior or disadvantaged in any way. For years, the Tullahoma school system used a standard elementary school report card that allowed the teacher to grade the students on subjective, behavioral issues such as co-operation, attitude, getting along with others and that sort of thing. There is one particular trait in which the Willis kids consistently received high grades. This infuriated our mother, and was guaranteed to put her in a bad mood on report card day. The high marks were for a category called "Persevering in Spite of Handicaps." We didn't understand her negative reaction to an A plus at first but she would tongue lash every one of those teachers. *"What kind of handicaps do those people think my children have, anyway?"* Eventually, they changed the wording of that, but after they took out the word "handicap" I stopped getting A pluses.

At school all of Mamas' kids did have a level playing field, if not a distinct advantage. First of all, we all liked school. School had clean bathrooms, plenty of toilet paper and hot water. Our house had none of that. The toilets were private, unlike the swinging bathroom door at our house. When our friends complained about the cafeteria food, we ate it for them. We were hardly ever absent from school. Most of us had perfect attendance records, and not just for one or two years. We were never sickly or whiney. With all the sniveling and complaining of some of the other kids, it wasn't difficult to gain the teacher's favor. Some of these teachers had come up the hard way themselves, and weren't making enough money to keep a small bird quiet, so they didn't have much patience for whiners.

For me, at least, the physical part of education was a piece of cake. We could do anything from standing on our heads to shinnying up a telephone pole. I knew eight different sets of rules to any game that included a ball, and I didn't even need the ball. I could play it with a rock. If the teacher was out of the room, I could hit her wastebasket from 20 feet away with a rolled up piece of paper. When you live in a neighborhood with a dozen barefoot, shirtless urchins of all sizes, you have to fight for your place in the pecking order regardless of your age. You have to prove yourself every day. Scratches, cuts, bruises... bring 'em on! The outdoors was my domain. It was hard for me to believe that some kids hated recess or gym class. To me, that was the best part of school.

Mama ran a mild-mannered household and her children carried that attitude to school, so we got along with just about everybody. We didn't know anything about learning disabilities and attention deficit disorders, but looking back, there were a few wild cards in every classroom. These kids were just considered unruly. Dyslexia wasn't a concept that anybody had ever heard of either. These kids were just considered slow learners. Children with poor hearing or poor eyesight might reach adulthood before anyone ever discovered their problems. and how they had to "persevere in spite of those handicaps." Many of these kids were held back a year or so through no fault of their own. There was no testing to identify their problems. The Willis family was lucky to have dodged most of those bullets.

I learned early that one of the best ways to get along in relationships is to share the abundant humor that life has to offer. Most of my social life revolved around competitive neighborhood sporting events. If you were to compete, at least in my neighborhood, you had to learn how to survive in the trash talking, dog-eat-dog politics of the playground world. But I wanted to do more than survive; I wanted to rack up an occasional win. And winning against bigger, older rivals requires a crafty game plan. What you might be lacking in age, size or experience, had to be offset with cunning. It was a battle of wits out there, and you could not afford to be totally unarmed. A good sense of humor can be the best gun in your arsenal. A well delivered wisecrack like, *"Smooth move, Exlax,"* could get a big laugh and temporarily stagger an opponent twice your size, no pun intended. There is a downside to this wisecracking tactic in that it only works about half the time. The rest of the time you are not only going to lose the game, but get your butt whipped afterwards. Over time, however, this dramatically improves your timing and your foot speed.

Humor has always been an excellent pressure relief valve. Mama wasn't drop dead funny, but she could diffuse a downhill situation with a well timed one-liner that put everything back into perspective, more of an attitude that anything else. If she burnt the only bread we had, she would explain, as she scraped the black from it, that she did it on purpose because she likes her toast that way. This was a common occurrence by the way. With all the things this woman had on her mind, she almost always burnt the toast.

One of the brightest of my classmates was the perennial president of our class and probably the smartest kid in our school. He was always trying to get us to quit clowning around, and he thought we would all be better off if we took things more seriously. He made straight A's in everything, and eventually went on to become a chemist with DuPont. This would have been the dream of a lifetime for any of us, but one evening he went out in his garage, sat in his car with the motor running and quietly put himself to sleep forever. I wish we would have told him not to take himself so seriously. "C" students don't do that sort of thing. When I reflect back on all the times that I experienced problems in my life, there seemed to be one common denominator. I was taking myself far too seriously. I was always more attracted to funny people, who seemed to have a more balanced perspective on life.

Donkey Softball Games

Once every year or so, one of the civic clubs in town would sponsor an event called a Donkey Ball Game. These shenanigans took place at the high school baseball diamond about a block from our house. Prominent business men, community leaders and local athletes would volunteer to make complete jackasses of themselves in a mock softball game played on the backs of donkeys. Each player stood beside his assigned animal until the batter made contact with a pitch. The batter then had to jump on his trusty steed, and ride to first base before the outfielders could mount their assigned donkeys and chase down the ball. You get the idea. Neither the players nor the donkeys had been trained for any of these antics, and the resulting mayhem could be enormously entertaining, at least for about an hour or so. Some of these men had never seen a donkey before, much less ridden one. The dysfunction factor could reach stratospheric levels. As the old saying goes, *"It's all fun and games until someone loses an eye."*

All the neighborhood kids wanted to go to these circus-type shows, but the admission fee was pretty steep. Charity or not, we didn't have that kind of money, at least not to spend on entertainment. But good ole Tullahoma (you have to love this town) had a standing rule. At the half-time of any sporting event, or midway through the game, they ceased charging admission. After that, anyone could get in for free. That's pretty much how I, and all my friends, got in to most of those sporting events. Whatever we could save on the ticket, we could spend at the concession stand.

The football field was adjacent to that baseball diamond. It was called Wade Field, named for Wallace Wade, Hall of Fame footballer who coached Clarke Military Academy in Tullahoma, and later put the University of Alabama on the map, long before Bear Bryant. Wade Field was lighted for night-time play, and all of Tullahoma's home games were played there. The stadium was surrounded by a formidable, 10 foot high, board fence that discouraged admission-free entry. None of us could scale a wall that high. However, there were a couple of loose boards on the backside of the perimeter, and we made sure they stayed that way. There were at least two occasions where those loose boards were worth their weight in gold. Tullahoma High played their football games on Friday nights and Davidson Academy, the Negro school across town, used the field for their Thursday night football games. The bright lights lit up the entire neighborhood on game nights and you could hear the announcer clearly from our front porch.

I'm sure they had a good reason for it, but Davidson Academy and Tullahoma High never played each other, and it's a good thing for the white boys that they didn't. "DA" had good teachers and coaches and their principal was probably the most well educated man in the community. Their football games were like a track meet with scores in the fifties and sixties. Between the halftime performance, the cheerleaders and the athletes, it was the best show in town, and the games were full of razzle-dazzle. DA normally won by a wide margin. Even their public address announcers were funny and entertaining. The Black community in Tullahoma had played an important role in the growth of the town since the war, and it was a big part of the town's history. The city elders probably didn't want to stir up a hornet's nest by getting a rivalry started with Davidson

Academy and that was probably a smart decision for that era. By keeping the two schools neutral toward each other we could all pull for both teams without any bias, which is exactly what we did. Anybody that could walk or crawl to those Davidson Academy games made sure to be there. I'm not going to apologize for sneaking into those games, because those were some of my best memories.

Tommy

My role model older brother, Tommy, tried his best at being an entertainer in his high school days. He was one of those characters who carefully planned comedy routines rather than depend of spontaneity. His premeditated pranks were simply a way of getting attention, and he quickly gained a well deserved reputation as a mischief maker. He liked to work these little one act plays alone, and enjoyed complicated pranks that had plenty of shock value. His classmates looked forward to his next drama, because it usually had an edge to it which bordered on expulsion from school. This presented the additional challenge of staying one step ahead of an unforgiving faculty. For example, where most people saw road kill, Tommy saw a terrified coed standing in front of her locker screaming in horror. There's some shock value. The weeklong investigation as to who put the dead possum in there was an added bonus. Then the "crime scene" had to be roped off for the intense faculty inquisition. There was little question as to who the chief suspect was, but there was no actual proof, nor were there any accomplices to rat him out. A few days later, the chalk outline of the dead critter was living proof of the old adage that the guilty party could not resist returning to the scene of the crime. Tommy 2, Faculty 0. *"Let's close this case before it gets nasty."*

Tommy could also write comedy. I had to listen to some of it. Whenever there was a need for an emcee, a school program skit or a microphone opportunity, he got the nod. If anyone was going to make a fool of himself, it may as well be Tommy... he had earned it, and he welcomed the challenge. His quest for the spotlight was somewhat of a contradiction, since his academic interest leaned more toward left-brained subjects like medicine and math. He had a fascination with etymology, especially big, argotic medical terms. He once asked me if I would like to know the longest word in the English language then proceeded to teach me how to spell Floc-cinaucinihilipilification. It has 29 letters, he told me, three more than the alphabet. Its #1 status has since been replaced by much longer, fabricated terms, and I have forgotten what he told me it means, but the fact that I even remember that word is a testament to his talent for capturing your attention and holding it. Maybe that was the only purpose of many of his antics, simply to give you something about him to hang on to.

Tommy was a dichotomy of thespian and scientist with little interest in sports. He had sort of a double personality like his daddy, intro-spective or extroverted depending on the moment and the mood. I think he knew for a long time that he would join the Navy, but only as a means to an end. Joining the Navy held the promise for college assistance through the G.I. Bill.

Sara was an athletic tomboy and entrepreneur. I think she knew for a long time that she wanted to be a nurse. I was an entertainer and an athlete. I was just trying to hang on one day at a time in the hope that something would come to me. Maybe I would be a writer. A talk show host! There were several guys in my class that were very bright and knew exactly what they wanted to be when they grew up, but it made me uncomfortable to hang out with them. They weren't very good at shooting pool, and I don't think they were very impressed with my eeny-meeny-miney-moe system of decision making.

Each one of us was stumbling to our own little bongo beat, trying to create a footprint that might lead to somewhere. For Tommy, Sara and me, time constraints caused by part- time jobs, friends, school and personal interests didn't allow us to spend much time together. Sara and I did have some great times picking blackberries in the summer, shooting hoops, and being traveling buddies. Tommy was five years older than me, and had his own agenda and friends. I didn't spend much time with Tommy and his pals, but when I was around he never let them kid me or belittle me for being a squirt. When Tommy spoke to you, he always made eye contact… an extraordinary trait, for any teenage boy. He seemed to be in a big hurry to grow up and become a Humphrey Bogart. He smoked cigarettes, and would do that thing where he spanked the pack on his wrist before opening it. For some reason, I saw a big difference between sneaking a cigarette every now and then and just lighting up in front of God and everybody else. I was a jock, and we had a different set of rules that didn't include smoking. Besides, I couldn't have afforded cigarettes anyway.

I was fascinated with all the clever ways he could light his cigarettes. It seemed to be a one handed thing. With a wooden match he could strike it by scratching it with his thumbnail, or across the hip pocket of his trousers. He could fold one of the matches out of a book of paper matches and, with his thumb, flick it across the strike pad and "bingo," instant one-hand magic. He could pinch a Zippo lighter between his thumb and first two fingers, and snap it open. Sometimes, he managed to run his finger across that little flint wheel just right and "voila," Showtime! There was no sense in doing any of these match tricks unless someone was watching, so lighting up a cigarette became a spotlight performance and something to be proud of. All this was the opposite of what I was being told by my coaches and mentors. *"Your lungs are your engine. Take care of them."* Somewhere in the five year time span between us, our values were separating, and I was losing the connection with my role model older brother.

The Dairy Dip

In the midst of all this tomfoolery, something extraordinary was coming out of the ground right across the street from us. Call it serendipity or dumb luck, a man named James P. Richardson from Jasper, Alabama decided to move to Tullahoma and build a soft serve, ice cream parlor one hundred yards from our house. This was not in the high end of town. But cleverly, he had located his new business venture near the elementary school where we had also relocated. He knew that every kid in school would eventually get hooked on an after-school, ice cream cone.

We watched carefully as this 40' by 40' concrete block box was constructed. There were two large plate glass windows in the front of the building and one more on each side. There was a small sliding glass window for serving near the front door. One day we came home from school to discover that the whole building had been painted white, inside and out. It was getting close to completion, but what was it going to be? The men who constructed the place either did not know or wouldn't tell us. Don Shockley, a freehand sign painter, finally solved the mystery for us by painting two large colorful words on each of the four big windows…"DAIRY DIP."

As soon as I noticed any sign of human activity inside that building, I was all over it, asking questions. Finally, Mr. Richardson, whom we would later nickname "Rich," was ready for business. I was there when the first pristine, curly topped cone of vanilla, summertime heaven was pushed through that sliding glass window. Who knows, I may have been the very first customer. It was the purest, most beautiful thing I'd ever seen and it tasted like spun vanilla sugar.

Perfectly white, and with a toasted cone sitting under it, I can taste it now. The Shockley Signs had also explained the pricing, so I had my nickel ready. But Rich did not take the nickel. He said the first one was free. That was probably not a good idea. As I said, this was not the high end of town. Within a couple of hours the word was out, and the place was swarming with snotty nosed little kids with their hands out, some of them swearing that, yes, it was "*still*" their first time. This can be a hard sell when you still have ice cream on your face.

Rich soon learned that he would have to expand his product line and add counter service. Nickels won't pay the rent, not even in that neighborhood. Within a few weeks he had added milkshakes and sundaes to the menu. Then he began offering a variety of soft drinks, candies and snacks. Before long, the front door was opened for inside seating, a counter was installed, and the odor of burgers and fries wafted from that wonderful place. Sure enough, every kid in school had discovered the Dairy Dip. Grilled cheese sandwiches, chilidogs, and finally, real pit barbeque could be smelled from inside our house, when the wind was just right. It must have driven the animals under our house crazy.

Rich's barbeque was the best in town. He smoked the pork shoulders and Boston butts for several hours over oak and hickory coals. While they were still warm, he de-boned them and wrapped them in butcher paper. Then he put them in the cooler overnight before slicing the meat about three-eighths of an inch thick. He warmed the meat on the grill, and basted it with a little spicy barbecue sauce before putting it on a toasted bun. This must have been some sort of Alabama style barbeque. It was fantastic and wildly popular. His outdoor cooker was smoking day and night.

There was no air conditioning at that time, and the windows in our house were usually wide open. The barbeque smoker increased our hunger quotient by a factor of ten. It also increased his sales. Business was brisk, and on the weekends he had to add curb service to accommodate the increased traffic. This was a windfall to the Willis clan. All the boys worked there. Tommy became his short order cook and his right hand man. Tommy could do anything. There were dishes to be washed, windows to be cleaned, coolers to be stocked, curb boys needed, and most of all, burgers to be eaten. This was a huge step up from his part time pool hall job. The Dairy Dip became an after school hangout. There was work for every Willis who could look half-way presentable for the health inspector. Rich learned early to never let the health department inspector conduct his inspection on an empty stomach. That was basically the difference between a Grade A and a Grade B rating, which had to be displayed "conspicuously in a prominent place" on the wall. But Rich did have his rules: if you worked inside, you had to wear shoes. You also had to be able to answer the most frequent question asked, "*What kind of milkshakes do you have?*" I can still remember the answer, which usually had to be repeated because we said it so fast:"*Vanillachocolatestrawberrypineappleraspberrybutterscotchandcherry*".

It was just one long burst of flavor energy, and we took great pride in spewing forth that answer. The customers thought it was hilarious and requested that we repeat it more than once. Ironically that was the same answer for sundaes too, since he used the same flavorings for both. He didn't pay much, but the benefits made up for the low pay. My favorite joke was that when Rich hired me he told me he would pay me twenty-five cents an hour and I told him I would *take* twenty-five cents an hour. So we both lived up to our end of the bargain. He once heard me tell that joke to a customer, and I don't think he saw the humor in it. Rich was a tightwad. But he had to know he was feeding the entire Willis household. He was far from stupid.

Sometimes, if business was slow and his tiny helpers were just sitting around, he would tell us to go home, but to keep an eye out from our front porch in case things got busy. This way he wouldn't have to pay us a quarter an hour to sit around on his time. We didn't see the humor in that either. But in the long run, Rich was more like a surrogate uncle to us. We never gave him enough credit for helping us grow up, and I'm not sure he ever gave us enough credit for helping grow his business. I've learned a lot more about the power of gratitude since then, and what it means to people to say "thank you." I regret not expressing more appreciation to Rich for all he did for us.

All through his high school years, Tommy was working nights and weekends at the Dairy Dip as the 'chief cook and bottle washer.' He practically ran the place. He made sure that if additional help was needed that Rich would give his little brothers the first shot at it. As Mama's kids continued to grow, the financial demands increased. The never ending need for school supplies, shoes and clothing, transportation, groceries and other expenses took everything that all of us could muster.

AEDC, THE SPACE AGE

Space isn't remote at all, it's only an hours drive
If you can get your car to go straight upward.   Sir Fred Hoyle

A couple of years earlier something bigger than the Dairy Dip had landed in Tullahoma's lap, and by now, it was hotter than Rich's smoker. In 1949, Tullahoma was selected as the site for a rocket testing facility. Both during and after WWII, the crafty Germans had so impressed our war generals with their missile and unmanned weapons technology that the U.S. was more convinced than ever of the need for missile superiority. Our national security depended on it, according to the experts. The Germans had constructed an elaborate series of secret testing facilities in small rural areas. After the war, a unique wind tunnel had been discovered in a remote section of Germany, and it was dismantled for shipping to our own scientists at home. Recruiting German scientists to the cause, our government began the race for space. The need for testing facilities prompted a survey for suitable locations. Tullahoma's role in the Camp Forrest training program, along with plenty of available water and electricity from the local TVA facility had placed our small town on the short list. All of this was being reported in to the Tullahoma News, of which I dutifully carried 20 copies under my arm twice a week.

Tullahoma's political centers of influence mobilized their lobbying strength. Tennessee Senators Kenneth McKellar and Estes Kefauver were not without clout. Former State Treasurer John W. Harton (Martha's dress), also a huge land developer, was no stranger to Washington politics. Harton solicited A.H. Sanders, an engineer for the Camp Forrest project, to bolster their presentation with overwhelming facts and figures. Mayor Jack T. Farrar, a doctor, and

Buddy Martin, one of the world's best small craft aviators, also made several trips to Washington to help make the pitch.

On November 9, 1949, it was announced that Tullahoma was selected as the site for a wind tunnel and would become a major part of the space age. The project was originally named the Arnold Engineering Space Center, named for General Hap Arnold, considered the father of the U. S. Air Force. Tullahoma had its "wind tunnel." Over the years this would become a godsend to the little town that had been put back to sleep after the War. Equally important, the place that would eventually become known as AEDC (Arnold Engineering Development Center) would have a profound impact on every one of my brothers and sisters.

NEED FOR ENGINEERS

The clarion call for engineers to work at AEDC brought some of the finest minds to Tullahoma. Good news for me, they read newspapers. The University of Tennessee in Knoxville and Tennessee Tech University in Cookeville, cranked up their engineering programs in response. Tommy, and every other bright young man with a slide rule and an interest in science, wanted to be included in this exciting new space era. This phenomenon would be an economic boon to the community and to my family for decades to come.

Mama was thrilled when Martha came home from Nashville Business College and accepted a job in the missile and space research program at AEDC. This was a government job, and she had to take a civil service exam in order to secure a government employee rating as well as a security clearance. Her "boyfriend" George was attending Tennessee Tech University in Cookeville and was preparing to be a rocket scientist.

Mama Meets The President*

(Well…she didn't exactly meet him. But she got to go see him.)

On June 23, 1951, President Harry S. Truman came to Tullahoma to dedicate the AEDC project. Martha was apparently still enjoying her Miss Tullahoma celebrity status, because she was invited to be at the focal point of this Presidential reception. As part of her new government job, she was to clear all VIP'S, control seating and oversee security for the stage presentation. No one could be on Truman's stage without Martha's permission.

When Martha came home with a handful of tickets for all of us to attend this historic ceremony, Mama kicked into high gear. This was a once in a lifetime opportunity, and we were all going to be there. The tickets included reserved seats on the train that left the downtown depot around 9:00 a.m. Saturday morning. Mama had us there 30 minutes early. We had walked to town. The train was already there, and had been for some time. Volunteers were crawling all over the train, mostly pretty young girls. It was hot that day. The train was hotter. They had cold water, orange juice and little snacks like the airlines serve. We were impressed. Sara, myself, Tykie, Beau and four-year-old Linda sat near Mama on the train. We kept asking Mama if she wanted anything so that we could go over to those good looking volunteers and get more free cookies.

The rest of the day was somewhat of a bust. Even though we had reserved chair seats, we were too short, and we couldn't see squat over the heads of all those other people who were pushing and straining to see the President. We finally got out of our seats and fooled around in the back of the crowd, where we had more room to flail and wiggle. We had to hang around close to Mama, but as long as she knew that we could see the train to get back on it, she was fine. All I remember is the heat from the sun and the red construction dirt. But we all got to be a part of it, and Mama got to see her Democrat President. Truman was a plain talking country boy from Missouri, and I think she related to his style. He was also embroiled in a bitter controversy with one of his Generals. These stories had been helping me sell newspapers. Mama was pretty pooped by the time we got home, but she was no stranger to rigor. We had to wear our Sunday shoes and clothes so you can imagine how glad we were to be home.

TRUMAN AND MACARTHUR

If you don't remember what happened between these two, the following is a short recap; once again, according to the newspapers under my arm. Truman had placed General Douglas MacArthur in charge of overseeing Japan at the end of WWII. In 1950, he also led the United Nations Command forces defending South Korea against the North Korean invasion. Truman was still smarting from criticism of the two bombing decisions that killed 230,000 Japanese. The President and his popular General were locked in a controversy as to how to proceed in the Korean conflict. MacArthur displayed obvious insubordination toward his Commander-In-Chief by publicly criticizing Truman's strategy, which the General considered weak. This was all a bunch of politics stirred up by some Republican Senators who were throwing fuel on the fire for the next election. The General wanted to cross the 138th Parallel, and storm the North

Koreans for a quick and decisive win. Truman felt that this action would cost needless lives and bring the Chinese and possibly Russia into full force against us. In April of 1951, President Truman relieved MacArthur of command. Instead of going quietly, the arrogant General chose to use his enormous popularity, and the perceived weaker position of the Democrat President, to rally Republican support and seize the day.

He was a brilliant and articulate speaker and was allowed to have his say before a widely publicized Senate hearing. The majority of the country rallied behind his charisma initially, but in the end, his egomania was his undoing. The American public finally saw through his Hollywood sunglasses, and found the real MacArthur. Over the next few months, his own Generals exposed him as a power monger, if not a complete nut case. The old soldier did fade away and did not return. Truman had come to Tullahoma to dedicate AEDC just two months after firing MacArthur.

Not to be lost in this "forgotten war" is that nearly 40,000 U.S. soldiers died in Korea, and 100,000 were wounded, mostly under MacArthur's leadership. More than 1,750,000 U.S. servicemen served in Korea from 1950 through 1953.

By now Russia had developed its own nuclear capability. The two Superpowers, the United States and The USSR would be locked into a Cold War for the next four decades.

To offset the Russian threat, Truman had established the Civil Defense Program and the Strategic Air Command

(SAC) to control land based bomber aircraft and our ballistic missile nuclear arsenal. All this was heavy stuff for a 10 year old. But this is the kind of stuff that sells newspapers, and that was the business that I was in. Mama liked

MacArthur at first, but she was a Truman fan, and Truman wasn't as keen as the General on stirring up a broader war after his experience with Japan and those atom bombs.

With four sons, and with teenage Tommy getting bigger every day, Mama couldn't help but remember her three younger brothers in WWII, and she was a handwringer. The last thing she wanted was another war.

***

Those next three or four years, when I was between 11 and 14 years of age, were some of the best years of my life, and I've had some good ones. We didn't have much of anything, but we sure enjoyed what we did have. I made my own spending money and my lunch money. I played on several ball teams, and made several new friends. I listened to my favorite singers on the radio and sang along to my heart's content. In my mind, I sounded just like everybody I sang with.

I learned to play sophisticated gambling games like far-away bottle with a Coca Cola. Back then, the bottom of a six ounce Coke bottle had the name of the town (where it was bottled, supposedly) imprinted on it. If two or more people got a Coke, the person whose bottle was the "farthest away" would have his drink paid for by the others. We learned this from watching the adults who played it. Grown men thought nothing of gambling for a soft drink, but for a kid to have to shell out to buy his buddy a drink was a very big deal. There was a geography lesson in this as well, because none of us knew where any of these places were, and we usually ended up in a loud argument. The game also promoted some very clever cheating, such as prearranging the bottles, which became another clever game in itself. We eventually determined that we were not suited for this game and went back to drinking Double Cola, which was bigger, and had no town on the bottom.

We discovered a better use for an empty soft drink bottle when one of my buddies had a birthday party and invited some girls. They introduced us to a game where we all sat in a circle, and took turns spinning the bottle. This was a far more civilized game, which also involved a lot of squealing and protesting, but without the girls, it wouldn't have had much of a point to it.

We made up games and reasons for games, most all of them ending in loud arguments. If we had old tires to slap around we would roll them down the street, steering them with our hands, believing that we were a truly awesome presence. We called ourselves the Terrible Tire Terrors. We may have slowed down traffic, but we rolled for justice. Super Heroes with big tires! When it rained, and the harder it rained the better, we stripped off our clothes and rolled up our skivvies into bikinis. We then rode our bikes around town like we were some sort of vigilante group. Our handmade flag told everyone that we were the Half Naked Outlaws. That's just about as bad as an outlaw can get, I guess. We hardly qualified as a gang because anybody silly enough to go along with this nonsense was automatically a Half Naked Outlaw. The novelty wore off quickly because, normally, where you find a summer rainstorm, you also find lightning. I can't think of many things worse than a couple of Half Naked Outlaws being killed by lightning, and being taken to the morgue with dirty underwear! Mama obsessed over our underwear a lot more than we did, as though we were always just one car wreck away from causing her almost certain embarrassment. But in our defense, I never once read in the Tullahoma News that a kid was in an accident, and his underwear was even mentioned.

"Young Johnny Jones was injured today when he was struck by an automobile while trying to stand up on his bicycle seat. He was taken to the emergency room for examination, and his underwear did not pass inspection. His mother was arrested and taken in for questioning."

One Saturday morning, me and the Hardaway kid next door, told the other kids that we were going downtown to rob a bank, and that when we got back we would all be rich. Robbing banks has always been a popular movie scheme. We were just bored and needed some creative entertainment. Our plan was to go by the police station in town and ask one of the policemen to hold a gun on us so we could have our picture made with my new Brownie Hawkeye. Then we would fabricate an outlandish story to go with the picture. The policeman at the front desk said he didn't know about all that, but he'd go get the chief. While we waited for Chief McEwen, we thought this might not have been such a good idea, and we might be getting a stern lecture from the head man. Instead, "Lo and Behold" the chief came out of his office, whipped out his pistol and asked "Barney Fife," the desk clerk, to take the pictures. We all had a big time, and afterwards they invited us back to see the jail cells. Must have been another slow day! It was Mayberry RFD in real life. We came home and made up a story for the other kids that the cops sniffed us out and arrested us. Then we told them that we were released from police custody for lack of evidence, since we actually didn't get a chance to commit the crime. Nobody believed any of this, but when the pictures were finally developed, with the Chief of Police himself holding a gun on us, our stock rallied for a couple of days. The biggest problem was the length of time it took to get enough money to pay for getting the pictures developed. The story lost some of its credibility during that six week lapse between the perpetration and the proof. By then, everybody had forgotten Act I of the play. All the grins in the mug shot gave the bank robber scheme away, but I still have that wonderful picture.

My family lived in that animal house on East Lincoln Street for eight years. The rent was $32.50 per month. It never changed. After that, I don't think anyone else ever lived in it. Later, it was torn to the ground. Horace, Martha and Ann all got married while we lived there. It was there that we got our first telephone, our first electric stove, our first refrigerator, eventually a TV, and Horace bought his first car. Beau and Linda started first grade while we lived there.

Baseball was the neighborhood game of choice because it could be played with just about any number of players. If there were less than eight players, then someone needed to pitch for both teams. A pickup game had no set number of innings, and we usually continued play until one of four things happened: 1. We broke our only bat; 2. Somebody got hit with the bat; 3. Darkness, or most likely; 4. Our only ball got lost in the high weeds. Those last two things pretty much went together. The only person willing to do more that a courtesy search for a lost ball in high weeds in the dark was the kid who owned the ball. Everybody else bailed early, *"Supper time!"*

Chiggers, mosquitoes, cockleburs, and an occasional tick were our natural enemies and we had little choice but to freely let them have their way with us. We had only one defense, to keep moving until we were so tired that we fell into a sleep so deep that we couldn't feel them itching anymore. I don't know if insect repellant had been invented, but I know we didn't have any. If you got a tick, someone had to hold a lit cigarette close enough to get the tick to let go. You weren't supposed to just yank it off and risk leaving part of the embedded insect under your skin. That could be big trouble. Everybody wanted to be the hero, but Tommy usually got to be the cigarette witch doctor, and he received a temporary, medical smoking waiver from Mama for that purpose.

She also enlisted his tobacco medicine-man skills on bee stings and ear aches. Apparently, if you pinch off the tip of a cigarette and wet it, the tobacco soothes the bee sting when applied by the right sorcerer. People swear by that one. Mama's country ear ache remedy was pretty bizarre, and you had to be steeped in witchcraft to let Tommy blow cigarette smoke into your ear from about two inches away. Few things are worse than smoker's-breath to a kid. That folksy remedy might explain the origin of the term *"blowing smoke."*

The telephone systems had undergone some improvements by the time we could afford one. We didn't have to call a central operator anymore, but we did have a party line. The service was cheaper if you shared it with other users. A private line was expensive. The party line presented some interesting privacy issues. You never knew who was listening to your conversation. If you needed to make a phone call when another family was on the party line, you simply waited an appropriate amount of time, and then interrupted their conversation by asking them to please let you make a call. Pity the person who had to share a phone line with the Willis household, where there was a line of people waiting to use our own telephone. Horace needed to have a phone because he was courting pretty heavily by now, and his work at the newspaper also had its emergencies. He was the only good reason we had a phone. He needed a vehicle for both those very same reasons.

**

When the rumor got out that Horace was looking to purchase a car, we could hardly contain ourselves. This would be our first car, ever. Somebody came up with the bright idea for all of us to help buy the car by "pitching in." We put a quart Mason jar on a shelf in the kitchen and enthusiastically bought into the program. Anyone who had extra coins would throw them in. Every day, Tykie would climb up there and get it down to count it for us to see how much it had grown. Our collective life's savings were in that jar. Somehow, $27 comes to mind. Even six year old Linda tossed in her penny collection. On top of that, when Ann came home from Nashville she put an entire paycheck in the jar. That represented a lot of peanut butter and apples. Little did we know that he was planning to get married and move into a place with his new wife, and take *our* new car with him.

This whole savings process only lasted a few weeks until one day we noticed that the jar was empty. Tykie went berserk. Who had taken the car jar stash? It had to be a bold, inside job. Mama explained that Horace had taken it and had gone downtown to purchase the car. Relief that we weren't going to have to kill one of our own for stealing the money, plus the excitement of the new car, was too much for little Tykie. He was bouncing off the walls.

We waited up as long as we could that night, but we went to bed without seeing the car. We didn't realize that Horace had a lot more to do than just get a car and spend the rest of the day showing it off to us. He had to go to work first, and then, he had someone more important to drive around that night. The next morning the car was sitting in the driveway: a brand new 1953 green Pontiac. We were all over it, in it, on top of it, under it, waiting for Horace to wake up and take us for a drive. There were a million dirty fingerprints all over that car when he finally woke up. The little ones could go for days without wearing shoes, and those dirty little feet made a more lasting impression than their dirty little hands. I'm sure he was delighted. Whatever new car smell that Pontiac may have had was short lived. We still got our inaugural ride, but he kept the car locked and the key closely guarded after that.

For all of his skills as a surrogate parent, Horace was never like a brother to me or any of my other brothers. His best friend was more like his brother. They fished together on weekends. Charlie Whitaker was a couple of years older than Horace, and worked with him at The News. Charlie was a good looking guy with a great personality. He was married and had a couple of kids. Charlie must have been a pretty good fisherman because they always came home with a big string of crappie or perch, and sometimes a big largemouth bass. Charlie and his buddies also introduced Horace to frog gigging. Gigging was a nighttime thing, performed with a strong flashlight and a long spear with a three pronged gig on the end. They gigged bullfrogs as big as dinner plates, and Mama fried the legs just like chicken. Charlie told us kids that it was hard to cook frog legs because they kept jumping out of the pan. We believed all that of course, and pictured them jumping all over the kitchen. He had a confidence about him that told me that he was the one who knew where the fish and the bullfrogs were, and that Horace was the student. We never thought of Charlie as being black or white or any color. That's why it was funny when he brought his little pig tailed girl over one day and some of the kids were surprised that Charlie would have a black child. What did they expect? He *was* a Negro. Somehow, we had forgotten about that.

Horace Gets Married

Soon after the green Pontiac arrived, Horace brought his future bride to meet her new family. Good luck! Marie Wilson Hodges, from Decherd, Tennessee was a divorced mother with a young child. Jimmy Lance Hodges appeared to be about five years old, about one year younger than our sister, Linda. The boy had a detachable brace on one leg and a crutch under each arm. He was one of hundreds of thousands of kids stricken by poliomyelitis. Every mother and child in those days lived in fear of polio, and Jonas Salk's vaccine had only recently been discovered.

We were prepared to spend an uncomfortable afternoon carefully entertaining this crippled youngster, even after Horace told us, *"Don't let the crutches fool you."* Sure enough, within a few minutes we were all playing ball. This kid had thrown down those crutches and could run like the wind. I'd never seen a kid love baseball that much. We kept looking over at Horace to see if this was what we should be doing with him. Horace had a big smile on his face, too. Jimmy never stopped running. Horace and Marie got the necessary treatment for him to make a complete recovery. He went on to become one of the best athletes in Tullahoma, and made his new step daddy proud. I don't think I've ever seen that boy without that big grin on his face.

A few weeks after the car came home, Horace was married. He took the car, our baseball player, he took Marie, and a very dependable source of revenue with him. It was time for him to have his own life, I guess. God knows, he deserved it!

A couple of years after that, Tommy graduated and joined the Navy. He and a friend, Wally McDowell, joined under the Buddy Plan which allowed two friends to be stationed together during their three year tour, assuming they make the same choices along the way. They didn't, of course, and they were soon headed in different directions. This Buddy Plan was a way for the Navy to lure more warm bodies into the service. The boys might need a little hand holding at first, but then the Navy would make men of them. That was the idea anyway. The GI Bill allowed educational benefits for veterans, and the boys were both looking for ways to get their college degrees later on. While in the Navy, Tommy was able to explore his medical interest and was trained as a medical corpsman. A corpsman is similar to a paramedic in civilian life. He had the unusual distinction of being temporarily assigned to the U.S. Marine Corps as a medic, which meant he was issued two different uniforms. I got the idea that he was proud of that distinction and that he favored the Marine uniform over his Navy outfit, even though he did not have to endure the rigors of Marine Corps boot camp. I asked him once if he ever ran into any floccinaucinihilipilification, or had to perform any cigarette voodoo at Camp Pendleton.

Tommy's military career path was following almost identically in the footsteps of his first cousin, John Harlan Willis. John was the son of my daddy's oldest brother. John Harlan left home to enlist in the Navy in November 1940, following an argument with his dad. John received corpsman training at Norfolk Naval Hospital, and was attached to the Fifth Marine Division at Camp Pendleton, the same outfit as Tommy. John and his Marine Corps unit participated in the battle of Iwo Jima. On February 28, 1945, in the heat of the battle to capture the island from Japan, John was wounded, and ordered back to the battle aid station. Disregarding his injuries, he returned to the front line to assist other wounded Marines. He was helping a fallen soldier inside a bomb crater when the enemy attacked with hand grenades. After throwing eight live hand grenades back to the enemy, he was killed when the ninth exploded in his hand. Heavily outnumbered, the Marines who witnessed this were so inspired by his selfless behavior that they rose up in spite of tremendous odds, and rallied to seize the day with hand to hand combat. The men gave credit to John for their inspired victory.

John Harlan was awarded the Congressional Medal of Honor, one of only eight give to Tennesseans during WWII. His posthumous citation is printed in the official publication for Medal of Honor recipients, and can be read in detail from the internet. John Harlan, like most soldiers, found himself in that life or death situation because of a choice he had made, and when he found himself face to face with his ultimate decision, he did not shrink. He was one of the men that Tom Brokaw spoke of in his book, <u>The Greatest Genera-</u>

tion. Men like him are the reason we are still reading and writing in English, and not using the metric system. I would have loved to have attended that funeral service but I was only four years old, and wasn't included. It would be interesting to know more about the emotional toll that John Harlan's death took on my daddy and his brothers and sisters, because it was less than two years later that my alcoholic father deserted my mother and her nine children.

Tommy had hardship allotments taken from his paycheck and sent home to Mama throughout his three-year tour of duty. If he could prove to the Navy that his being away from home was a hardship for his family, the government would match a portion of his allotment check. Proving hardship was not a problem. This allotment practice was very common among servicemen then, and still is today. The military has always been a blue collar enterprise. Tommy enjoyed the bravado, independence and travel opportunities of his service tour. He was all grown up now, and like his daddy before him, he enjoyed the company of more than a few drinking buddies. Thankfully for Mother, he was never exposed to combat duty like his cousin, John Harlan.

Praise

I had a horrible education. I attended a school of emotionally disturbed teachers.
    Woody Allen

Maybe you grew up in a generation that lavished praise on their children. Most of my generation did not. This is a concept that must have come along later. We didn't get praise, and, therefore, didn't expect it. You had to "interpret" praise. If you were being treated normally, that was praise. You were doing ok. If you were being ignored, then you were being sent a message. This subtle ostracism would continue until you overcame it with as much acceptable behavior as was necessary to offset the offense. You were expected to know what that was without being told. Today, that kind of psychological bashing would be called passive aggressive behavior, but fifty years ago it was called parenting. And it worked. I personally thought it was better than getting whacked with a stick.

Mama never laid a hand on me. The way she corrected her children was by saying something subtle like, *"Let's make sure we never have to go through anything like that again."* She might have smacked me in the butt with a straw broom (my fake guitar), like that would hurt, but she wasn't real touchy-feely with her kids either. She never just came over to me and gave me a big hug and said, "I just love you to death," or anything like that. The way she showed her love was by being there. Every second of every minute of every hour of every day Mama was right there for us, twenty four seven! She didn't take a smoke break because she didn't smoke. She didn't go down to the local bar....she didn't drink. She didn't duck out for a drive...she didn't drive. She was there when you got home from school. She was there when you got home from work. She was there when you were sick, and she was there when she was sick. She didn't learn this from a book or a TV talk show. We didn't have a TV. She learned it the same way she learned how to roast a Thanksgiving turkey. It all came from Bluestocking Hollow.

With her boarding house of nine, Mama had to listen to more than her fair share of homework over the years, and she had a pretty good education in her own right. Somehow though, we all knew that she was not the go-to-gal for upper level algebra problems. She did have her own little reservoir of book knowledge that she could shock us with on occasion. One night when Ann was working on her physics homework, she came upon a question that asked for a term to describe the pressure that a (certain) material can withstand before it snaps. Mama was ironing and listening at the same time when she mumbled, *"Everybody knows that."* Since nobody else in the room seemed to know the answer, we all looked at Mama to see what her punch line would be. The joke was on us when she instantly blurted out the correct term, *"Tensile strength!"* What a great physical principal for a woman in her position to know, because it could be used to define her.

She was always ironing. I was the only one in the room with her one night when she was ironing and deep in thought. I guess she had been through a particularly rough week, because she suddenly muttered out loud, *"Well, just damn!"* It was the first time I had heard her use anything close to profanity, and I had to ask what she said. *"You heard me, just damn!"* Poor Mama, she didn't even know how to cuss. The incongruity of this made me laugh. We both started laughing, but she must have apologized to me three times that night and again the next morning. She seemed to want me to understand that it was not really her that said that.

Selling Papers

The key to success is under the alarm clock.
  Benjamin Franklin

Would you like to guess as to the two worst things about selling newspapers when you are 12 years old? Well, the first answer is rain: cold, wet, miserable penetrating rain. Snow is not a problem. People like snow a lot better than rain. When it snows, everybody's in a good mood. When people are in a good mood, sales are good. Rain is the opposite of that. Snow is fun and people love to get out in the snow, but even if you are hopelessly in love, singing in the rain is a myth. Gene Kelly and a handful of Half Naked Outlaws are the only persons ever to do that. Rain dampens newspaper sales for more reasons than one. Nobody likes a wet paper.

The second worst thing involves having to get out of a warm bed in middle of winter. For starters, getting up before daylight is not natural for a sixth grader. (That's why kids pee in the bed, because they hate to get up.) I only mention this so you will have a small appreciation for how much one or two dollars a week meant to me back then. That amount of money was the lost opportunity cost of not getting up before daylight, at least for a paperboy. If you add the two things together, having to get out of a warm bed to then going out in the cold rain, you will know what I mean. There was no one to wake me up, or coddle me into making this effort. I either did it or I didn't. Skipping a day of newspaper sales, rain or shine, would mean that my customers would be buying their newspapers from my competition that day. They might get used to that. That simply was not an acceptable alternative.

My family had a cheap alarm clock that we passed around, and I played games with it by setting it ahead 10 or 15 minutes to fool me into thinking it was later than it was when it went off in the morning. Then I would have that extra few minutes to lie there in that glorious state of being ninety percent asleep. That trick never really worked, because the ninety percent somehow turned into one hundred, and then there was no backup plan. You can't cheat time! I finally resorted to having the all-night dispatcher at the Checker Cab Company call to wake me up so that I had to get all the way out of bed to answer the telephone. The cab company was my free wakeup call service. I still don't know why they did that for me.

Sometimes, when I got back home from my two hour paper route, I would learn that schools were closing that day due to extreme weather conditions. As much as I enjoyed hearing that news, I couldn't help but be amused that I had already ridden my bike past the school twice that morning. But what did I know? After those papers were sold, there was no greater feeling than knowing you had those coins in your pocket. Everything else you might be faced with that day would be a piece of cake compared to that. Every kid should be lucky enough to experience that feeling.

In all those pre-dawn bicycle raids on the shoe factory, I had to learn a few short cuts for those days when I was running a little late. The hypotenuse of a right triangle may be shorter than the sum of its two other sides, but it's not necessarily a smoother ride. The shortcut involved crossing a set of railroad tracks, carrying my bike across a few ditches, and cutting through some back yards. In the 1950's, people didn't care if you cut through their yards, especially if you were a hardworking paperboy on a bike. In fact, if they saw you through the kitchen window, they smiled and waved. You might have to avoid a few dogs, but usually most of them were still asleep when I came by their house. The railroad tracks are not the most desirable place to locate a house. These were hard working, blue collar people on that end of town, and they were looking for value. A little train noise was the least of their problems. I was surprised at how many lights were on before daylight, especially near the tracks. This was the real America. I could smell breakfast cooking, and it smelled so good that it made me ravenous. I swore that when I grew up I would get up early in the morning, before daylight, and cook a big breakfast with bacon and eggs that smelled that good.

There was a correlation between the time I got to the shoe factory with my newspapers, and the amount of money I took home. It's all about that "early bird" parable. The factory workers punched in at 7 o'clock, and really had no reason to get there earlier than that, but about 20 of them did. It was pretty much the same 20 people every day. I figured these were the achievers. They were the ones in the best mood, and most of them bought a paper. The few who ran late were also pretty much the same ones every day. This group didn't have time to stop to get a newspaper, because they always ran late, and they didn't seem to be in as good a mood as the early birds. This information is not included in the "bird and the worm" parable, but it was a pretty handy little piece of information to have if you wanted to get rid of those papers. Most of my sales happened early or not at all.

By the way, when I got older, I tried that pre-dawn bacon and egg breakfast thing, and nearly gagged. It just wasn't the same thing. I never had a good breakfast growing up, and, from habit, it is still hard for me to hold anything substantial under my nose until about 10:30 in the morning. After that, I'll eat anything.

Snow

The first snowfall of the season was not just an event, it was a magic show. Snow was, and still is, the great common denominator that transforms young and old, rich and poor, into Christmas elves. I remember making a little fist and rubbing a hole in the frost on the window to stare at the streetlight to try to see how hard it was snowing. What would be waiting for us the next morning? How deep would the snow be when we woke up? *"Snow harder, faster, more, more!"* I talked to the snow as my warm breath frosted the hole again. *"C'mon, baby!"* Nothing compares with that giddy feeling of weightlessness as you anticipate the spectacular holiday that awaits you tomorrow: hot chocolate with marshmallows, snow forts, laughing and sledding and who knows what else. Everyone would certainly be in a happy, holiday mood, and if anyone had any minor guilty indiscretions against them, this was atonement day. Maybe we could make some snow cream if the snow was clean enough. (Many homes burned coal furnaces and there was sometimes a thick layer of black soot in the air.) No matter what had happened before, a good snow day would wipe the slate clean. Everyone would start fresh again. All bets were off. All sins would be forgiven. Love was in the air. A free ride! Such was the childhood miracle of snow.

The next morning everybody huddled around the radio to hear the verdict, hands held in mock prayer. *"Please, please, please, please! No school."* Mother smiled at all this as she burned the toast. She remembered what it was like. Everybody remembers. Finally the school board verdict comes in, as if they were having a big meeting somewhere; every kid's worst nightmare, *"Schools are open today."* Borderline expletives in every room of the house, and in 10 minutes the place is empty. Turns out it didn't matter. We went out in the snow, walked to school and had a great day. It still felt like a holiday.

At school, the teachers gave us the good news that we didn't have to have an extra day tacked on to the end of the school year, which made us all feel more grownup and responsible. After a few days the snow became a filthy nuisance, but that first snow day was the most fun you could have for nothing. You can't buy that kind of excitement. On a good snow day, you could make friends with people you didn't even like. When we got home, Mother knew we would all be cold and wet from making fools of ourselves, so she had the hot chocolate ready.

You could play outside in the snow as long as you wanted but once you came back inside, that was it; you couldn't go back out. That was the rule. Inside, the snow would melt, and your clothes would be wet. Going back out in wet clothes was apparently a recipe for a bad cold or, who knows, maybe polio. But mainly, every time that door was opened, the heat flew out. Mamma didn't like a cold house, and we didn't want polio either.

Middle Tennessee is located on a meteorological fault line if there is such a thing. Canadian cold fronts treat the Kentucky-Tennessee state line like a weather DMZ. The cutoff line seems to be just north of Nashville. It can be snowing a blizzard in Kentucky while people are playing golf in Tennessee. If Abe Lincoln truly did grow up in a cabin that straddled the Kentucky state line, he saw an awful lot of weird weather. Being right on the cusp of every single winter storm meant that we never knew how to prepare for what may or may not be coming. It drove the forecasters crazy.

Most people don't know that Pat Sajak (Wheel of Fortune) got his start doing the weather for Channel 4 in Nashville. He is the first funny weatherman I ever saw and he admits that he knew absolutely nothing about the weather. His broadcasting career took him from Nashville to L.A., where there is no weather. I could have done that. But it doesn't matter who tries to predict the weather in Tennessee, it simply cannot be done. This phenomenon presented some freakish incidents including an unexpected ice storm in the mid 50's that finally answered the question about that huge oak tree in our front yard.

SARA GOES TO NURSING SCHOOL

Nurses are angels in comfortable shoes.
   unknown

With Tommy's enlistment into the Navy, Mama had successfully graduated four of her finest from under her roof, but still had five to go. Fortunately for her, the Korean Conflict had settled down to a stalemate, and Tommy was not being exposed to live hand grenades at Camp Pendleton in California. It was a good thing Truman fired MacArthur, I guess, or he might have been in a bomb crater in North Korea.

Ever the entrepreneur, Sara was finding opportunities that were more fitting for a 15 year old than being a papergirl. She was babysitting for the owner of the downtown movie theater when she was offered a job as the concession manager. This was a fantastic bluebird for the rest of us. It wasn't long before she had made some arrangements for us to see certain movies for free, if they weren't sold out, which was seldom; and she even had connections with the popcorn concession-aire. All we needed was a dime for the Milk Duds (yes, they went up in price too), and we were good for a double feature.

She worked that job at the Marshall Theater throughout her high school years, and became the most self-reliant of any of Mama's kids. But being in the entertainment business had some serious drawbacks. Sara had to work nights, weekends and special occa-sions, which are the exact times that people have spare time to watch movies. So, while everyone else was playing, Sara was working.

One story that we love to tell on Sara happened on Thanksgiving Day. Most people had the day off on that special family occasion. Except for Sara! The Marshall Theater had matinee movies starting at 4 pm that day, and she had to be there around 3:30 pm to set up her concession stand. Mother had prepared a traditional Thanksgiving feast, which was to be served as our one and only meal of the day. Normally, the dinner would have been served around 2 pm, but Mother insisted that we all eat together, and we had to accommodate all the teenagers' afternoon social activities with boyfriends. So this was to be a 3 pm feast, cutting it a little close for Sara, and also stretching the boundaries of the boys' appetites. It doesn't take that long to wolf down a Thanksgiving dinner, but someone came up with the bright idea that we should all go around the table and say something that we were thankful for. I had been hanging around the turkey and knew about this little "family workshop," so I had my *good health* speech all ready. The little kids and even some of the older ones were caught cold in their moment in the white-hot spotlight, and between the gratitude and the giggling, this whole process was taking a lot longer than it should have. The clock was not the only thing ticking for Sara as we plowed our way through this clumsy exercise. When it finally came around to Sara's turn to express her sincere gratitude for all that life meant to her, she had reached the boiling point. She stood up, threw her napkin down in her untouched Thanksgiving dinner plate, right into the giblet gravy, and announced that she was *"Not thankful for a damn thing."* Whoa! Cussing and everything! This was high drama. Then she stormed out of the house, slammed the screen door, walked to town and worked until nearly midnight. We all understood her plight, but we also knew she would get over it before she got halfway to town. Unwittingly, she had given us all something new to be thankful for:

a great story that we could tell on her for the rest of our lives. She also left a nice plate of food that the boys quickly divided among themselves. Mother fixed her another plate, and put some "tin foil" over it. It was warmed up and waiting for Sara when she got home. She knew that would happen, and we all knew that nothing needed to be said about her outburst.

"Not thankful for a damn thing!" Boy that was a good one.

Sara was a terrific basketball player. Her only experience was playing against the neighborhood boys, and she had never even played against girls before, and girls played a half court style back then. Her girlfriends didn't even know she could play basketball until they had intramural games at school, and Sara scored at will. She scored more points than the entire varsity team averaged. With all her pent up frustration, no one wanted to step in front of Sara when she was driving to the basket. The girl's varsity team wasn't all that hot at the time, and the coaches begged her to play on the school team. But she couldn't afford that luxury. That took way too much time, and she had other priorities. She was the next to leave the nest, and instead of being a drain on family resources, she was a substantial contributor. We never gave her enough credit for that.

After her graduation in 1956, Sara went to Saint Thomas Nursing School in Nashville, and became a Registered Nurse. She took a nursing job in Miami. When she started sending home pictures of herself and her girlfriends laying around on boats in their swim suits, her mother was not amused. Mama began some behind-the-scenes maneuvering to get Sara back to Tullahoma. She found out that there was a job opening at AEDC, and she arranged for Sara to be contacted and interviewed. This worked out well for everybody, and

Sara would come back to her hometown, and eventually find her an engineer. All new employees at AEDC had to report to the nurse to make sure their shot records were up to date, so Sara met just about every person who worked there. But mainly, Mama had her cash cow back home where she could keep an eye on her.

TRIAL AND ERROR

The biggest problem with raising kids is that it doesn't come with a complete set of instructions and by the time you know what you're doing, you're out of a job. Mama was using the make-it-up-as-you-go method, and was flying mostly by the seat of her pants. There was somewhat of an "us against the world" mentality with all the odds seemingly stacked against a single mother with nine kids. Inflation was running rampant. We had no automobile, no major appliances, no adult paycheck, and one of her kids needed something just about every 20 minutes. The poor woman had a tiger by the tail.

Ironically, our country was in a similar trial and error situation with our new President, Dwight Eisenhower, who was trying to make some sense out of the mess our country was in. He got more than he bargained for in trying to lead our growing democracy against formidable Communist adversaries, mainly Russia and China. Eisenhower had a military mindset and ran the country with a soldier's mentality. One of his achievements was the creation of an interstate highway system, designed specifically so that long, five mile stretches of straight "runways" could serve as emergency airplane operating areas during wartime. This was not an original idea, as the ever clever Germans had planned their Autobahn system for that same purpose. But it's a perfect example of how many political decisions were being driven by military thinkers. A great deal of thought was being given to the idea that someday we might have to defend our own turf, just as England, France and Germany had recently been forced to do.

Somewhere in all of this paranoia, the Superpowers must have concluded that it was better to find alternate battlefields to settle national differences, rather than fight on their own turf, so that they wouldn't have to ravage their own cities in the process. The battle between North Korea and the "Republic" of Korea, under Truman's regime, gave the Superpowers just such an opportunity. They were able to rattle their antlers on the world stage by pitting Communism against Capitalism, but they staged the fight in someone else's backyard. In combat, apparently, there is no such thing as home field advantage.

Russia gained the most from the Korean chess game and invested the least. They raped the North Koreans of much of their commodity resources in exchange for air support. Stalin's side of the bargain with North Korea was for Russia to receive 9 tons of gold, 40 tons of silver, 25 tons of lead (annually) and 15 tons of monazite (nuclear ore).

Most people don't realize that wars are fought over assets, not ideology or political differences.

Stalin's dead numbered only 316 while Mao Tse Tung lost 1000 times that many men in Korea. The U.S. asked for and received nothing from South Korea, while sacrificing over 40,000 soldiers. Mao Tse Tung is considered by most historians to be the biggest mass murderer of the twentieth century, being responsible for as many as 38 million deaths, primarily his own people. Stalin's reign of post-war ethnic cleansing and deportation could have accounted for even more, but the secrets of that country are too cloaked in secrecy, and the numbers are so great, we will never know. We do know that he deported over three million of his own people to Siberia. Poor Harry Truman was just a country boy from Missouri who dropped a couple of little bombs that killed 230,000 Japanese civilians. He was practically a Boy Scout compared to Mao and Stalin, but America still had a hard time letting Harry live that down. This was the crazy world we lived in during the "Happy Days," and little Number Six (me, if you've lost track) had no idea how soon I would be plugged into all this.

I would have to wait a few years to find out firsthand how history can repeat itself. In a few years China had cut a deal with North Vietnam to raid the rice farmers in South Vietnam and confiscate their surplus rice. There was enough surplus rice in South Vietnam to feed a lot of China's hungry people, and it was considered the bread basket of Southeast Asia. Not many people are aware, then or now, that the Vietnam War was fought over rice. And there was at least one more thing that we did not know at the time. That little food fight had my name written all over it.

America is a large, friendly dog in a very small room. Every time it wags its tail, it knocks over a chair.
    Arnold Toynbee

America has done a lot of mind boggling things since 1776, and many of them happened in the Fifties. Some of them affected rich and poor alike. One of them happened in the shoe store. Buying a new pair of shoes was a big deal for a youngster because shoes were expensive items. Boys wore high top Keds or PF Flyers that cost about two dollars a pair, and they usually fell apart before we outgrew them. They had virtually no arch supports. If they were too small, or hurt your feet, we would cut slits in them to get a little more mileage. Girls wore saddle oxfords or penny loafers. The younger ones of a large family wore other people's shoes that were handed down. In other words, our shoes never fit. If there was a special occasion when the kids needed a new pair of shoes, we were not allowed to purchase them on our own. We had to be accompanied by an adult, for fear the salesman would sell us a pair that actually fit. The ideal shoe for a 13 year old might be two sizes too big. This way he could grow into it over the next year or so, and the shoes wouldn't be obsolete by the time he got home from the store. That's how fast our feet grew, I guess.

They had a new machine at the store that would x-ray our feet. The salesman encouraged all the kids to go over and stick their feet in and wiggle their toes around. This new sales gimmick was nothing more than an entertainment "WOW" to lure customers in to the store. Sure enough, you could see the bones of your little feet and the outline of the new shoes. This thing was called a fluoroscope and everyone was free to use it as much as they liked. The problem was that it was emitting dangerous, low level radiation. It turned out that many shoe salesmen developed cancer of the gonads from standing near those machines in the normal course of their work day. Eventually, it was determined that this machine was a frivolous sales ploy, and that it was totally unnecessary to see your toe bones in a pair of shoes, so they scrapped the whole idea and got rid of those machines. The health hazard was never mentioned. Fortunately for me, I had a sister in the x-ray business and she warned us to stay away from those things. So thanks to Ann, I still have my gonads.

Another great American Fifties story concerns fluoride. Totally unrelated to fluoroscopes, fluoride was even more dangerous until they got a handle on it. Highly poisonous to begin with, huge quantities of fluoride were needed in the production of the atom bomb (over there in Oak Ridge, Tennessee). Some scientists decided that there were practical benefits to this fluoride product especially in the dental area, but they weren't sure about the application. The number of Americans who were killed, or whose teeth fell out from these experiments, is one of the deep dark secrets of our nuclear past. This was all part of the Manhattan Project, and that embarrassing part of the record is mysteriously missing.

Since most of these fluoride experiments were conducted in rural communities, many farmers were direct victims. A big cloud over the local fluoride factory was not a blessing for the local crops, or for the air quality. Hopefully, the crops died before the poisonous food was eaten, but that was not always the case. They finally got a handle on all this, and settled on the practice of putting trace amounts of fluoride in our drinking water. Each municipality was on its own in administering the proper dosage of this lethal poison to our drinking water. Since it was dangerous to handle, you can only imagine some of the unfortunate, hourly-waged people who drew the short straw on that assignment. (The minimum hourly wage was one dollar at the time.) A little too much fluoride in the water caused white spots on the teeth. This was called fluorosis, and we saw plenty of that in the Tullahoma and Coffee County school system.

In spite of all this trial and error, fluoride in our drinking water and in our toothpaste, was considered one of the top twenty public health initiatives of all time, but at what price we will never know. It is still a controversial subject among some scientists, who feel that fluoride does not magically attach itself to our teeth and nothing else. Relative to all the danger that lurked around us, I would give my mother high marks for having enough sense to keep our family healthy during these experimental times. But we had no way of knowing the toll that all this was taking on her. All too soon, that would become very clear.

New York City
November 13, 2008 10:15 a.m.

As we watched the monitor in the NBC green room, they were showing a CNBC segment with a pretty brunette interviewing Jim Cramer about the stock market. Cramer (Mad Money) had been blindsided by the bear market like everybody else in the business, but suddenly he was taking heat for some remarks he had made, telling people it was time to take some money off the table, meaning liquidate or sell. This was the equivalent of yelling fire in a crowded theater. Mad Money was more than a catch phrase at this point. Just about every investor was furious with their brokers for not giving them better advice on taking care of their assets in this current debacle. Money was a sensitive issue and Wall Street was not a happy place right now. New York wasn't all that much fun because of it. Manhattan is normally a great place to visit unless you happen to be there on business, then you are forced to be on somebody else's schedule. Lee and I like to wing it when we travel. I've worked hard all my life, and was a slave to the clock for so many years, that now I don't even like to make a golf tee time if I don't have to.

All the vocation tests that I ever took in school steered me into only one area: *sales*. Unfortunately, the only things that I had ever sold were newspapers, milkshakes and an occasional magazine for a school fund drive. Little did I know that this would be the perfect resume to eventually land me a successful 34-year career in the securities business! No wonder Wall Street was so screwed up. You'd think they would hire finance and business majors.

I wasn't comfortable with all the things that I witnessed in the securities business. Not the least of which, is that they would pay an English major for dispensing investment advice to adults. I quickly learned that many CEO's prefer having English and History majors on their staffs on the assumption that they can read, write and communicate, which is what business is all about, after all. Our industry packaged every conceivable product to be sold as investments, from Ginnie Maes to office buildings; you name it we had it. They shrouded the risks in thick, legal offering memorandums (prospectuses) that nobody read or understood. The great majority of these investments actually worked, so that the process fed on itself until the need to feed the greed eventually created such outrageously fabricated products that neither the buyers nor the sellers understood their risks. It was like force feeding a goose to make fois gras. The charm of something for nothing has always had enormous appeal.

The thirty year fixed mortgage, the stud horse of the financial world and the backbone of our economy for decades, had been mutated, sliced and diced into so many confusing, highly-leveraged packages, that not even the bankers knew the risks that these hybrid securities represented. So, when real estate prices dropped sharply for the first time since the Great Depression, the result was wide sweeping and devastating. Finally, in the third quarter of 2008, Humpty Dumpty fell off the wall, and there wasn't anybody alive who knew how to put him back together again. Even Alan Greenspan, the former Fed Chairman was dumbstruck. The barbarians were at the gate, and they were sacking the treasury looking for their money. All they found in the empty safe was a hastily prepared, hand painted sign with two big words scrawled across it: *"Money's gone!"* They had killed the golden goose, and only a few feathers were left.

The markets had imploded. Stocks, bonds, municipals, commodities, oil, real estate, everything had come unraveled. Wall Street would never be the same. As Warren Buffet likes to say, *"When the tide goes out, we get to see who's been swimming naked."*

Apparently everybody had been, and it was not a pretty sight. Many good companies had lost half their stock value seemingly overnight. Bank stocks appeared to have no bottom. Oil, which had reached 150 dollars a barrel, suddenly had dropped to below 50.

When Wall Street sneezes, the whole world catches a cold. The bloodletting was relentless. Our own investment bankers had done what Bin Laden could not, they brought down the world economy.

It was crashing down around our necks. Wall Street had securitized everything that wasn't nailed down; and packaged it in bales of greed so large that, when the end came, the losses were monumentally catastrophic.

Fortunately, for me, I was on the outside of the tent looking in, and I had the benefit of knowing that they were still hiring ice cream salesmen. I also had the advantage of some of Mama's inherent, Bluestocking wisdom, and I could see the arrogant excess that usually precedes a steep correction. About a year before the whole ball of yarn started to unravel, I had already begun my retreat. I sold many of my stocks, except what I thought was too good to sell. I found out later that there is absolutely nothing this is too good to sell.

Every asset class was hit and hit hard. There was no real end in sight. Stocks go up because of earnings, and in this environment, I didn't see where earnings were going to be coming from until the economy returned to normal, and that was going to take more than a new President with a crafty campaign slogan. Half our money was gone, and it had taken a lifetime to earn that money, so this recovery was going to take a long, long time. The government was putting together a huge bailout plan for the banking system but to me it looked like they were just rearranging the deck chairs on the Titanic.

It was hard to enjoy New York in this environment. I didn't want somebody jumping out of a tall building and landing on me. I fantasized briefly that Kathie Lee and Hoda would interview me about the market on the show. Why not? Every other idiot in the world had given their opinion. Back to reality, in a few minutes we would do our show: and afterwards, maybe Lee and I could enjoy the true spirit of New York.

Buddy Takes His Turn At Bat

...and the time came when the risk it took to remain a tight little bud became more painful than the risk it took to blossom.
  Marcus Aurelius

I was the first one of Mama's kids to be born in a hospital. We lived in Gallatin Tennessee in 1941. Midwifery was common in the Forties, especially where money was an issue. A year or so after I was born, Pete took his family from Gallatin to Tullahoma to work as a butcher. Before the War was over in 1945, I would have two more brothers.

I was a shy little Buddy for a long time and spent most of my time observing and listening. I had separation anxieties when I wasn't close to home. I didn't overcome this until I was a teenager. Several things happened to me when I was in the seventh grade that caused a big change in me. West Junior High was a couple of miles away, and I had to ride my bike to school. A teacher named Ms. Hill asked us to write a story each week using 25 newly assigned vocabulary words. Instead of writing a different story each week, I decided to write a serial story with continuing chapters, a concept I had picked up from my Saturdays at the Marshall Theater. This was a novel approach that I hoped would get some extra credit for creativity. I got extra credit and then some. The stories took on a life of their own.

My narrative involved two bumbling burglars who sat around in their garage apartment smoking cigars, evading the law, and planning their next bank job, which they always bungled in whatever way the vocabulary words allowed me to make up the story. Ms. Hill thought this was hilarious, and had me read my tale aloud to the class each week. Since the other kids had to struggle to get the same words into their stories, every time I spoke one of the assigned words in my reading, the kids would howl with delight over the novelty of it all. The Friday reading of my "next episode" soon became something the entire class got excited about, and I had to ask the teacher if she would mind changing my reading to Mondays, so I would have the weekend to make the story funnier. She agreed without hesitation. Once she even told the class that if they didn't settle down, she was going to punish them by not letting Buddy read his story. As convoluted as this weird threat struck me at the time, I was smart enough to realize that it was my first taste of power. It was a little scary, but I loved every minute of it.

That was when I knew I wanted to be a writer. I loved the reaction from people from something that originated solely and completely out of my own imagination. This was fascinating to me, and I wanted more. I learned later that appreciation is the deepest craving of human nature, and it was an epiphany for me. Being appreciated and accepted for something that comes naturally is the ultimate high for a human being. I would also learn that there are no unrealistic goals, only unrealistic time frames; and it would not be my destiny to wallow in the luxury of getting paid for what I loved to do. At least, not for a long, long time. I would have to settle for something I didn't like as much in order to get a paycheck. Sound familiar?

There was a boy in that seventh grade class named S. W. Stone. He was a very popular guy that I had never seen before. He would say outrageous things that other people wouldn't dare say out loud. The way he laughed about it, as though he was hearing it for the first time himself, made it even funnier. He was a one-of-a-kind, completely original comedian, and I was smitten by his comic delivery. We became fast friends and remained that way. He gave me the confidence to express thoughts that were different without feeling self conscious about it. I found out later that just about everybody has weird thoughts from time to time, especially the kind of people that I enjoy being around.

This group of guys had a different culture than the ones in my neighborhood. They traded knives, and talked about cars they liked, and some they had even driven themselves.. S.W.'s family owned a grocery store, and he worked there on weekends and after school. Later on, he was one of the first kids our age to have his own car. It was a 1946 Ford. When the windshield wiper came on the whole car waggled. Just about every car was a stick shift back then, and he taught me how to drive in that car. Sometimes it needed to be pushed to get it started, and we doubled-dated in it a lot, sometimes having to push it with the girls in it. We had some hilarious times together.

I discovered something else during that coming of age period when I played my first game of organized basketball. I found out how much easier a game can be with an actual referee. We played an intramural game, which is a fancy name for indoor recess during cold weather. I scored more points than all the others on the floor combined, largely because none of them had ever had to play in my neighborhood with the Hardaway kid hanging all over them. After the game, when I changed from my gym shorts, I noticed that my hand-me-down boxer underwear was longer than my gym trunks, and had been hanging down below them the entire game. I cringed for the harassment that was surely in store for me. But, when I walked back into the classroom, I got a whooping and hollering standing ovation. I was being appreciated yet again, and the shorts were never mentioned. Maybe it isn't the clothes that make the man. Nowadays, everywhere I go I see kids with their underwear hanging out, but I started it.

There have been several disappointments in my life, but I never dwelt on them. One of them stands out in particular. Chewing tobacco! I anticipated nothing more than my first opportunity to have a big wad of it in my jaw during the first baseball game of the season as the starting left fielder at Tullahoma High. As soon as I put it in my mouth, I realized something was not quite right. After we took the field, and the first ball was hit to me, I made a scrambling effort, and when the play was over, I realized that my wad was missing. Where did it go? I must have lost it in the heat of battle. I looked around the place where I caught the ball, and there was nothing. I'd swallowed it of course, and both my stomach and my head soon confirmed that news. Death could not have come soon enough. It took me a long time to forgive the Indians for introducing us to that vile plant. Another monumental, personal catastrophe was my first taste of "chitlins," which I had heard a lot about, and was anxious to give them a try. I knew exactly what they were, but I was curious to know how they really tasted. Like the chewing tobacco, I wanted to see if I was a real man. When I finally got the chance, I tasted them twice, once going down, and once again coming back up. My first and last chitlin!

INFLATION

Inflation seems to have only one law, whatever goes up will continue to go up. This insidious rule wears hard on the incomes of the hourly-waged, especially when it's only 25 cents an hour. All those years that we didn't own a car, gasoline was between 15 or 16 cents a gallon. I remember this from cutting other people's yards in the summertime.

The customer would provide us with the lawn mower but didn't supply the gas. For an average size yard, two guys would get two bucks and split it. The problem was the gas. We couldn't even net a buck apiece. The first thing they always told us before cutting the yard was, *"Don't run over the flowers."* Well, the Weed Eater hadn't been invented yet, and it was a heck of a lot easier to mow down a few buttercups than to pull all those weeds out by hand. We weren't smart enough to be more aggressive with our pricing, and, therefore, we got exactly what we deserved. And so did the customer. The two bucks was for mowing, and that's exactly what we did. Those flowers were going to die anyway.

For almost one hundred years, it cost two or three cents to mail a letter in America. Sometime in 1956, the postage stamp increased to four cents, and never looked back. Since then, the U.S. Mail has been a reasonably accurate inflation index. As of this printing, it's 43 cents, roughly 10 times the 1956 cost. Everything else increased accordingly. If an automobile sold for $4,000 in 1956, there is a good chance the sticker price would be a little over ten times that today, or around $43,000. A $40,000 house might be closer to $430,000, and so forth. Using this general rule, gasoline shouldn't be much more than $2 per gallon today. The recent drop in crude oil prices from 150 dollars to less that 50 dollars a barrel (November, 2008) put the price of a gallon of regular gas back down to about two bucks. So, at least for the time being, justice was served.

There is one popular All-American product that has somehow defied the laws of inflation. I still remember the day they changed the coin slot on the Coke machine at York's Grocery from five cents to six cents, and added that extra slot for the penny. The original Coca Cola bottle held six ounces, which meant that Coke, at the time, was a penny an ounce. I have seen three liter plastic Coke containers on sale at the supermarket 50 years later that sold for 99¢. There are approximately 100 ounces in a three liter bottle, so if you do the math from that perspective, Coca Cola can still be purchased for a penny an ounce. If you know of any other product that can make that claim, please tell me now. The biggest drawback of this convoluted logic is simply this: there is no way that the three liter Coke is going to taste as good as the six ounce Coke did fifty years ago. The fact that I would rather have the six ounce Coke than today's three liter bottle tells me that they have changed that product somehow. I can't find anyone close to my age that won't agree with me. Once you pour the first glass out that big bottle, you might as well pour the rest down the drain, because it will be flatter than a pancake in 5 minutes.

In the early Fifties, the Baby Boomers were getting into Scouting and Little League baseball, and there was an increasing demand for more and more "Boomer" products. Anything that had to do with an emerging population of little kids was a hot commodity.

We lived in a town that made baseball bats and baseballs, so business was booming at Worth Manufacturing in Tullahoma. One of

Mama's brothers worked at Empire Manufacturing in Shelbyville, Tennessee, and they made No. 2 pencils by the tens of thousands. This new Boomer economy also gave us a rude introduction to inflation. When the Tullahoma News went from a nickel to a dime overnight, I thought that was a good thing. I was a paperboy, not an economist. The price of labor, ink, paper and new printing presses were driving these decisions, according to my big brother. The News had just purchased a new printing press, which cut down on the time it took to print the paper but not the costs of printing it. It never occurred to me that everything else was going up in price, especially groceries. Mama's grocery sacks were getting slimmer. Nobody was quicker with a grease pencil than our grocer, Monroe York.

Inflation brings opportunity to those who are in a position to pass it along. Technology brought opportunity right into the living room. Television networks were beginning their relentless commercial campaigns, extolling the health benefits of self rising-baking powder, the cleansing power of Ajax, and the sweet smell of Palmolive soap. Ironically, every other ad was a cigarette commercial, extolling the virtues of Lucky Strikes or *Pall Mall, famous cigarettes! Outstanding and they are mild. You can light either end.* Ordinary people now had television sets and were being bombarded with these commercial presentations.

People came to our front door to sell Watkins Products, pots and pans and Encyclopedias. There was a whole new entrepreneurial world opening up out there, all spurred by this Boomer phenomenon and television. But we were slow to cash in on any of this action.

Little League Baseball was on the leading edge of this population wave. Worth Manufacturing hand sewed their baseballs, and used local workers to do this at home, in their spare time. There was a unique sign in front of the factory that advertised "Sewers Wanted." (I always thought that they could have found a better way of wording that sign.) With a few hours of free training, anyone who wanted to stitch baseballs, could take the parts home by the dozens, or by the hundreds, and bring back the baseballs whenever they were finished. As long as each baseball passed inspection, they were paid by the piece. For reasons unknown to me, Mama would not buy into this program. Maybe this was not the kind of sewing that she wanted to be associated with, but we sure could have used a few of those baseballs.

Baseball is a lot like fishing. People who don't understand it think it's boring, but for the people who do, every pitch holds the promise of high drama.

Me.

On October 8, 1956 something happened that has never happened before and is unlikely to ever happen again. The World Series was a radio event then, and whether you were in school or in a factory, it was un-American not to listen to every pitch. Stores would turn up the volume to attract customers. The New York Yankees were legendary. Their roster included names like Bobby Richardson, Yogi Berra, Mickey Mantle, Billy Martin, and Hank Bauer... the Bronx Bombers, as they were called. The defending World Champion Brooklyn Dodgers were called the Bums. Their lineup included Duke Snider, Pee Wee Reese, Jackie Robinson and Roy Campanello. If you get nothing else out of this book, go to a computer and Google the 1956 World Series and read about those seven games.

The Dodgers took the first two games, and it looked like a repeat of 1955, until the Yankee pitching staff delivered an unforgettable performance. It was in the fifth game when the miracle happened. A modest, no-name, 27 year old Yankee pitcher with a mediocre record took a three ball count on lead-off hitter Pee Wee Reese and never looked back as he went on to retire Reese and the next 26 Dodgers. It was the first no hitter in World Series history. This stood the sporting world on its head, and was the talk of every small town in America. The roof nearly came off the Dairy Dip. Not much got done at school that day. Don Larsen had lionized himself in baseball history, and he is a household name today. The highlights from the game were numerous, including near-miss foul balls and

Mantle's famous hit-saver, still known as "The Catch." Larsen's last pitch was a controversial, game ending 'call strike' by the umpire, that could have been a little outside. But before the Dodgers could get into a protest, the Yankees had cleared their bench in celebration, and Yogi had already jumped into Larsen's arms. Game over, a true classic! A single ticket stub souvenir for that game is now worth 2000 dollars.

Sporting events have always been a good bridge between the young and the old. I still love to watch the crowd at a baseball game, because the stands are full of little kids chewing on their baseball gloves, waiting for something spectacular to happen to them. Back then, if a man in the stands caught a foul ball, he would look around for a nearby kid with a glove, and flip it to him. I haven't seen anyone do that in a long time.

***

Throughout the Fifties, the movies made cigarette smoking seem like a sexy, cool thing to do. Professional golfers puffed cigarettes during major tournaments. Consequently, just about everybody had a go at smoking as soon as they thought they were old enough or could get away with it. If a young kid got caught with the smell of real cigarettes on him, he might be forced to smoke a whole pack, or a big, stinky cigar in order to teach him a lesson. This was supposed to make him sick, and therefore, never want to smoke again. At least this was the parents' logic. I know it worked with Red Man Chewing Tobacco.

Cigarettes were 20 cents a pack, or a penny apiece, and they seemed to introduce a new brand almost every month. Sample packs of four were offered as enticement to try out the latest new taste or the new filter-du-jour. These introductory samples were supposed to be free, and were clearly marked, 'Not for Resale.' But Rich made us charge a nickel for them at the Dairy Dip anyway; otherwise his allotment of samples would have been gone in an hour. Every kid in America had a hideout, and there was no better use for a hideout than getting together to puff a little contraband. In lieu of cigarettes, we would smoke corn silks, ground coffee, sage grass, or anything else that would stay lit in a piece of rolled up paper. Our favorite cigar was a long, dried bean from an "Indian Cigar Tree." It was really a Catalpa tree with long brown pods shaped like cigars. All of this stuff tasted awful, but it was the idea of smoking that made it an adventure. We had never heard of pot, thank God. Like Clinton, there was no inhaling. One or two puffs and you had smoked, and that was the whole point. Of course, you can't smoke without matches, and matches added a double feature no-no to our secret sanctuary. I offer this as indisputable proof that kids will try anything that they see in the movies.

GRUNDY STREET

The huge, formidable oak tree in our front yard was probably three feet in diameter when we moved to Lincoln Street, and it had added about an inch of girth per year for the eight or nine years that it guarded our empty dirt driveway and menaced our flimsy tin roof. Among other things, this tree served as our basketball backstop, and our home base for a game called "kick the can." When a totally unexpected, winter ice storm swept through the mid-state area in the middle of the night and quadrupled the weight of its limbs with a thick coating of solid ice, the root structure gave up the ghost. You could have knocked that tree over with a five foot jump shot. No one heard the fall, which must have happened well after midnight, while we were all sound asleep.

The tree fell exactly 180 degrees away from the house, taking down power lines and everything else in its path. Its mass was so great that it created a crater in the street in front of our house. I can assure you, that tree had never been pruned in its life. It was a big boy. It still had our basketball goal nailed to it; the orange hoop was crushed beyond what our little hammer could repair. The entire street was blocked for a couple of weeks. The scene literally made people gasp. The first unspoken thought of anyone who saw this monster lying in the street was unanimously obvious. It didn't need to be said, and it was not lost on my hand-wringing mother. We had not only dodged a bullet, as far as she was concerned, we had all used up one of our nine lives. Even though the ominous tree that she had worried might fall on us for so many years was no longer a threat, she decided that day that it was high time to move her cubs to higher ground.

The fear of such natural disasters seemed to haunt the dreams of poor people. The media and the movies had a way of compounding the frenzy by interviewing every little ole lady in curlers that every experienced a tornado. They always said the same thing, *"It sounded like a freight train."* We had tornado drills and fire drills at school. We even had atomic bomb drills where we ducked down and put our heads under our desks. Everybody knew that little desk was highly overrated, but we did it anyway. All these things just gave little kids another reason to pee in their pants when they went to bed at night. If we had ever had a fire in that house on Lincoln Street, the whole place would have burned to the ground in 10 minutes.

***

When I was 16, after my junior year of high school, I was enjoying a promising "career" as a small town athlete. It was popular then for boys to take summer jobs that were outdoors and physical so that we could stay in shape and be ready for the rigors of fall football. My girlfriend's father knew someone who got me a job with the city doing road work. I hated everything about the job, mostly because the regulars thought that I was a privileged kid and was taking a job away from one of their own. This was an ironic notion, but not entirely ridiculous, because in many ways I was privileged. I was also horning in on their good ole boy culture, which included shooting craps during breaks, sharing a half pint of Lynchburg Lemonade (Lem Motlow Sour Mash Whiskey) over lunch, and spitting Beechnut chewing tobacco all over everything.

Anyway, after three gruesome weeks of patching potholes with hot asphalt, they no longer saw me as part of their team. We were digging a sewer line at an elected official's house one Friday afternoon when the foreman gave me the news that they were laying off the summer help for budgetary reasons. I think I made 30 dollars a week, so I knew that was a crock. I walked home and took a bath, and wondered how I would tell my girlfriend's father that I had lost the job that he was so proud of getting for me. I was not sure whether I should be delighted never to have to work in that environment again, or be dejected over getting canned. I hadn't told anybody, not even my mother, but I knew I was going to eventually have to tell my girlfriend's father. Although she and I had to keep certain secrets from him, that would not be a good one to keep. As I was leaving the house that night for my Friday night date, the phone rang. Mama said it was the Commandant of Culver Military Academy in

Culver, Indiana. He said that he had received my application and the nice letter of recommendation from my high school basketball coach, Ken Trickey, and wondered if I could be in Culver on Monday to join their summer staff as a camp counselor. This was my first miracle. Even though I knew this would mean leaving my family and my girlfriend for nearly nine weeks of summer, that night would be one of the happiest nights of my young life. I never had to explain to anyone that I got fired. I just had to say I had been selected to go to Culver. Until now, nobody ever knew about the rest of the story.

Culver was great and I was good at it. Looking after clueless little rich boys ranging from eight to twelve years old, and teaching them basketball, rowing, paddling and canoeing on Lake Maxinkukee, was a piece of cake and a dream come true. I got one nice letter from my girlfriend that was curiously hurried and a second one about ten days later that was a predictable, one page dear-John. I found out later that the night I left for Culver, and we said our goodbyes, as soon as I stepped onto the train, she had a date that same night. (I wondered why she got dressed up.) She had no intention of waiting around all summer, and I really couldn't blame her. This way, she had someone to hang out with at the country club pool while I was having the best summer of my young life. I wasn't the country club type anyway. All's well that ends well.

I did pick up some valuable information from my teenage relationships that I will share with you. It's about trust. Nothing tears out a man's heart, young or old, and stomps that sucker flatter, than a good case of betrayal. It's like a drop of ink in a bottle of milk. Once it's in there, there is no way to back it out. Trust is a thin membrane, and once it's been compromised, the good stuff oozes out. Men place a very high standard on the women in their lives, and they have extremely fragile egos. I think all men feel this way, because, when it comes to women, we are all like little boys. Women may be able to forgive and forget, but the brain of a man is not wired that way. Once you are caught in a lie, you can kiss it goodbye. Even if a man continues a relationship, after being lied to, he will always keep a safe emotional distance. The bottom line is that men are just not mature enough to handle being lied to, even though they might do it to others all the time. I don't know how you are going to use that information, but you can't say I didn't tell you.

I went back to Culver Summer School for two more summers, and each year was better than the last. When I returned home from Culver in August of '58, Mama had moved to a new address. Maybe she was trying to tell me something. I had to ask directions to get home. The five hundred block of East Grundy Street was closer to town and only a couple of blocks to school for the little ones. We liked the new house, even though it was far from new, and it had its own unique set of issues. God knows, nine kids and nine years had pretty much done a number on the previous one. I went by the old house on Lincoln Street later, and the big stump of the fallen tree was still pointing away from that house, like a monument to what might have been. More than a year later, it still posed ominous challenges for my old tobacco-spitting road crew that would have chop it up and remove it.

Mama had whittled us down to only four by now, and it seemed like we had more room in that house, even though we actually had less, especially with Linda's piano relic sitting in the living room. In the fall of that year, I introduced my younger brothers and sister to all the new games I brought home from Culver, like Quoits, Badminton, Four Square and Frisbee. We had our own weekend mini camps and I was still the camp counselor.

"All glory is fleeting."
       General George Patton

All of a sudden I found myself the oldest child at home, and it was my turn to take the torch and see what kind of leadership I could bring to the table. This was going to be interesting. During my junior high school days, I discovered that I was pretty good at several games. Sports were like a big toy department to me. Somehow, from all those neighborhood free-for-alls, some skills emerged. Bringing home a baseball uniform to be washed was a new thing for Mama. Apparently they didn't have organized sports in Bluestocking Hollow. But thanks to her, we had the advantages that come from living across the street from a school system that had a complete sports complex.

When the city built a brand new high school across town in 1957, I played in the first football game to christen the new stadium. The *whole town* came out to be a part of history and to see Wilkins Field. Lo and behold, I scored the very first touchdown that night. Then we lined up for the extra point, and I happened to be the kicker, too. I had scored the first 7 points on the new field; a record that can never be broken. I had a great season opener, and we blew the other small school away. Life was good. Horace told Mother all about my *heroics*. While this was only my umpteenth ball game, Mother had never been to any of them, nor did she understand what all the fuss was about. It was all foolishness to her which wasn't going to amount to anything. She would have preferred to see me prepare myself for some sort of sensible career. She did come to one of my baseball games a couple of years earlier, and got there late, just in time to see me strike out. (That might have been the day that I swallowed the chewing tobacco.) She left immediately, and never came to another one. *"Take me out to the ball game"* was not a tune she would likely be humming.

Horace finally talked her into going with him and some of the family to one of my football games. He picked them up in his 1953 green Pontiac. Mother didn't have a clue about what was going on during the game, but she was fascinated by all the loud hollering going on around her, especially if my name was in the air. Somewhere in the heat of combat there was an incomplete pass, and she overheard one of the fans comment loudly that Willis should have caught that pass. (Yeah...well, get your butt out there and catch one.) On the next passing opportunity, the same local rednecks were shouting encouragement to complete the first down pass, when out of the blue Mama cups her hand over her mouth, and shouts, *"DON'T THROW IT TO WILLIS!"* This was totally uncharacteristic of her, and the rest of the family roared with laughter at her off-the-wall outburst. We won the conference that year, and went to a bowl game. But all of that, plus the fact that I was one of the captains of the team, was all lost on Mama. She had a way of keeping you humble. She showed her support in her own way, and always had a special dinner for me when I got home from practice. The truth is, she would have loved to have come to all those games, but the transportation issues, and fears of seeing her children get hurt, dominated her decisions. She couldn't bear seeing people get carried off the field. Besides, she had to distribute her attention evenly among all her children. Home was her stadium.

Nobody had to tell me that there was no better way to prepare for a life of competition than competitive sports, so it wasn't a complete waste of time. Sports opened some doors for me, but in the long run Mama was right, I wasn't going to have a career from it. I had a handful of minor injuries that didn't help her to see things more clearly either. She liked seeing my picture in the Tullahoma News, but even then would usually comment on my posture. I knew what she was trying to get across, and I just let it amuse me. She was such a good, sweet woman. We loved her to death, and she could do no wrong.

I was a pretty good team leader, but I'm not sure I was always leading in the direction that the coaches wanted the team to go. Bottom line, to me, sports were just games, and supposed to be fun. Once, when we were preparing for an important game, the coaches unveiled a new trick pass play designed especially for me. I was to fake a reverse, but throw the football down field. To introduce the play in practice, the coach tossed me the ball and said, *"Willis, do you think you can pass this thing?"* I don't know what you might have said if someone had set you up that perfectly, but to me there was only one possible response, it wasn't original, but I couldn't resist it. I looked down at the ball and then back at him and told him I didn't think I could even swallow it. I knew that was not the answer that he was looking for, but the players loved it. Now, there I was, one of the team captains, trying to help the coach prepare the team for a big game, and I just couldn't resist being a smartass. That play worked several times, by the way.

When our high school added track and field to our sports agenda, I tried every event, thinking I would excel in all of them. Turns out, you can't do all of them, because some of them are going on simultaneously. I settled for high jump, the 100 and the 200 yard dash. I always got points for those events, but they seemed to be over quickly and I was just standing around, bored.

The coach came over to me one day and asked me to run in the 880 yard run, because we only had one runner in the race and he thought I might be able to get third place and score a point for the team. Being a sprinter, I had never run a race that long, unless it was one leg of a relay. I felt a bit insulted by his backhanded compliment that I might be able to place third. At the first turn, I looked behind me and there was nobody within 20 yards of me. I was smoking the field. When I hit the straightaway, my legs started sending the message to my brain that this was not a 220 yard sprint. I could see a lot of real estate in front of me, and heard thundering hooves breathing down my neck. By the next turn, my legs felt like rubber bands and I started seeing old dead relatives. About 200 yards from the finish line, I pulled up, left my lunch on the infield, and could not even stand up for about 15 minutes. When I finally made eye contact with the coach, he had a big smile on his face. He knew. The bastard!

In the absence of a father, many of my coaches (like that one) served as role models. Coach W.C. Cooper was our football coach and he imposed a strict, ten o'clock curfew for the players during football season. None of us were really obeying the rule, so he pretended to have some snoops out checking on us, and accused us of not respecting his rule. We thought that was baloney, that there was no way he could know what all of us were doing. We just figured he wanted us to go to bed about the same time he did. One day the guys decided to challenge him on it, and the players asked the captains to call a team meeting. This curfew was cutting us out of some seriously good parties, and putting a crimp in our social life. It also gave the competition a leg up on the available dating pool. Even the girls' parents would let them stay out until eleven. We had our meeting, and invited Coach Cooper in to hear what we thought of his curfew. The coach was brief, and said he would be delighted to change the curfew, but with one condition.

"I'm going to leave the room for 10 minutes. When I come back, if you can tell me one good thing that happens after 10 o'clock that's good for this football team, then I will be happy to change the curfew."

Well, as they say in the locker room, he had us by the short hairs. We were stumped. We all looked at each other and realized that we'd been had. We all knew what went on after 10 o'clock, and it was none of his business. We didn't even call him back into the room. We just abandoned the meeting and smiled at him on the way out. At least he was smart enough not to check on us too carefully or he wouldn't have had a football team that year. He did lead us to the conference championship.

I had some coaches who encouraged me to play sports in college, and that was nice of them, but I soon found out that I needed to fill some good sized gaps in my scholastics. It was time to listen to my mother, and prepare myself for the real world. Besides, I had my bell rung enough times to know that donating my body to some college was not an intelligent choice for my brain, or my 175 pound frame. Like a lot of other small town jocks that got through high school on sports and charm, I had to hustle to get my high school and college education simultaneously. Then I took a cue from Sara, and worked a nice "low impact" job in a restaurant that paid my way through college, with no more broken noses.

I didn't mind not getting a full college scholarship, but some career advice would have been useful. The sum total of my career guidance went something like this. One afternoon during my senior year at Tullahoma High, I received a note that the Superintendent of Schools wanted to see me in his office. This was unheard of. I'm not talking about the superintendent in charge of the janitorial staff. This is the top dog, the CEO, the General himself. His name was actually Robert E. Lee, by the way. (I'm not making this stuff up). No student I ever knew had ever been called in by Mr. Robert E. Lee.

He sat me down, and talked about my family and my mother for awhile, and was extremely gracious. I thought he might be leading up to a big Oprah surprise, where I got a four year scholarship to Vanderbilt, or a car or something. I was on the edge of my seat. He finally asked me what I wanted to do after I graduated from college. I told him I planned to try to get through the first year and figure it out from there. Why not be honest? I did know that there were kids out there that knew exactly what they wanted to do with their lives, but I never ran around with any of them. So I waited for my surprise.

Instead of a prize I got a suggestion. He told me that he thought I might be very successful as a television entertainer. He then proceeded to offer not one single clue as to how I should go about doing this, so it pretty much died with the speaking of it. What a bummer! A nice career went down the drain.

If there is a moral to that story it might be simply this: kids will remember a compliment for the rest of their lives, even if it is a clumsy one. But more importantly, if you are going to give advice, be prepared to back it up with some practical information.

Allow me to illustrate the proper way to give useful advice to a young man entering college who doesn't know what he wants to do. Choose English as a major! Mr. Robert E. Lee might have told me that. But I had to figure this out for myself. English is required for the first couple of years anyway, and it's not like math. There is nothing subjective about math, if you can't come up with the exact answer to a math problem you are out of luck. Not so with English. Much of English is subjective. When your English professors see the English major beside your name on their class rolls, you will immediately be considered one of the chosen few. They will think you know more than you really do, and give you special attention, including credit that you don't deserve. After all, as an English guru you are one of them. But that's only the tip of the iceberg. Since mostly girls major in English, you will likely be the only guy in those classes. This is not a bad position to be in. I can only tell you what I know. Using this simple strategy, I made it through college in four years without flunking anything, became the Editor of the Campus Literary magazine, dated some very intelligent girls, and had three absolutely ridiculous poems published.

I worked nearly 40 hours a week in an off campus restaurant to get through college. I left home with $200 in my pocket and came home after the first semester with $206. As a freshman, I always made sure to schedule an 8 am class every day to force me to get up and get going. My older siblings taught me this. It was just like selling papers. I wasn't going to have the luxury of sleeping in. I had a long four year grind ahead of me, and I was no Einstein. I had to trade in my sprinter's mentality, and learn to pace myself for longer distances.

Most animal trails follow the line of least resistance, and that seemed to describe the path I was taking with my college classes. Thanks to a couple of high school teachers, I had less frustration in liberal arts than other subjects, so I followed that route. It was clear from the very first week on campus that I had not prepared myself properly for college. I had gotten through high school on sports and a little personality. The English degree chose me, because, other than quitting, that was the quickest way to a conclusion and a degree. Quitting was never an option.

Years later, I learned that the greatest value of a college diploma is that it proves to your employer that you have the ability to start something difficult and finish it. Employers also like the fact that Liberal arts majors can write and communicate, which is what business is about.

***

People have often asked me how I got the name Bud. Now that I am a writer I can finally tell the real story. When I was born I was given the last name of one of my father's drinking buddies, Beasley. There was a Mr. Beasley in the furniture business around Gallatin and Nashville. If you paid attention earlier, then you know that Pete doesn't do middle names, so I'm just Beasley Willis. This name has caused much confusion over the years, especially when the last name is given first, as it often is. Since Willis is a popular first name, I have often been mistaken for a person named Willis Beasley, of which there is more than a few. My name must also be difficult to read, because when I stood before my university president to receive my college diploma, he called me to his podium by the name, "*Willy Beasley.*" Our president was a well educated man, but even he could not handle my name. Six months later, when the Admiral in charge of the Naval Air station in Pensacola recognized me as a flight school graduate, he called 2nd Lt. Bilsy Willsey to the reviewing stand. Two of the main highlights of my life to that point were marred by my father's penchant for bestowing weird names. But it was hilarious, and a befitting tribute to the class comedian. The absence of the middle initial seemed to be the root of the problem. Don't do that to your kids.

No one wanted to call a baby boy by the name Beasley, so before I could walk, I somehow got the nickname "*little Buddy*" which was shortened to Buddy. This is the name that got me through high school. Later, it was shortened to Bud but not until I was a freshman in college. There was a beautiful redhead in my freshman biology lab at Tennessee Tech whom I met in the rest room. I had gone into the ladies room by mistake, and didn't realize it until I was washing my hands. When she came out to wash hers, she was real flirty, and said we should meet like this more often. I was impressed with her personality. In our next three hour lab session, I went over to see what she had under her microscope, and asked her for a date. She said thanks, but she didn't think she could go out with a guy named Buddy. She told me that she had a dog back home named Buddy, and her mother would think it was a scream if she was dating a guy with the same name as her dog. I told her she could keep the dog and call me anything she wanted, so we settled on Bud. After a couple of very long evenings with her, I found out she had more than a few issues that she had trouble keeping straight in her head, but I continued to use the name Bud because I didn't know how many other people out there might have dogs named Buddy. I later discovered that Buddy is by far the most popular name for a dog, and that there are almost as many of them as there are people named Willis Beasley.

Some people, like birds, are driven to activity. In the process, life happens. In the middle of my junior year of college, three upperclassmen came to my dorm room and said they were looking for a fourth person to sign up for Marine Corps officer training. *"A few good men"* was all they wanted, they said, and four was enough, according to them. Because all three were big men on campus…one of them was the quarterback of the football team, another was the president of the student body, and one was the Commander of the ROTC drill team, I swallowed the bait. A few good men, indeed!

Twelve weeks of platoon leaders' training at Quantico, Virginia was enough to convince me that I wasn't interested in being an infantry foot soldier. At the very first opportunity, I opted for flight school. At my college graduation from Tennessee Tech, I accepted an officer's commission in the Marine Corps, and then I was sent to Pensacola to become a Naval Aviator. Twenty months later, when I got my wings, I was sent to Jacksonville, N.C., to train for combat. We were eventually all going to be sent to support the Marines around Danang. I had jumped out of the proverbial frying pan and into the fire. But I did have the added advantage of vertical flight, and there was much to be said for that. Pilots don't usually have to sleep in the jungle at night, and the prospect of trying to sleep in the dark, surrounded by people who are trying to kill me, made flying into combat zones, even under fire, seem like child's play.

Pensacola

To put your life in danger from time to time,
breeds a saneness in dealing with day-to-day trivialities.
   Nevil Shute

The last thing Mama did before I left for flight school after graduation from Tennessee Tech in June of '63 was to put both her hands
on my chest and tell me in the sweetest imaginable way, *"Now Buddy,*
you be sure to fly low and slow." I smiled and gave her a big hug and
kiss, and then caught a train to Florida.

When I first arrived in Pensacola to report to the Naval Air Station,
I was smitten by the place. The weather was beautiful, airplanes
were playing overhead, the base was pristine, and men twice my age
with rows of ribbons on their chests were saluting me as though I
had done something special. I barely knew how to put on my uniform correctly. Before we were allowed to touch a plane, we had to
complete ground school. This amounted to about three months of
class work and testing to see if we had enough sense to have another
half million dollars spent on us before we got our wings.

Most of the class work was technical. Physics, Aerodynamics, Me-
teorology, Math, Engines, and Flight Theory were just a few of the
subjects that were thrown at us immediately. English Literature
was never mentioned. Most of the candidates were recently commissioned officers and college graduates from all over the country,
and they had been screened many times before they got to this point,
both psychologically and academically. A liberal arts graduate coming into this environment could have found himself in over his head,

and this English major certainly was. I had gone to one of the best engineering schools in the country, but had majored in English. But at least these aviation courses were written in English, and I could read and write, which helped immensely.

We were allowed to flunk a subject or two and retake it, but we would then have to drop back to the next class, which meant we could fall weeks behind schedule. All the exams had the same number of problems to solve, and a passing grade was 40 out of a factor of 50. All that mattered was passing or failing. Once you passed you went forward and your grade was forgotten. I can't tell you how many 44's I got but I never failed anything.

Some of the 14 astronauts chosen that year to participate in the Apollo program sat in on some of those ground school sessions with us. Buzz Aldrin, Alan Bean, David Scott and Eugene Cernan were part of that group, and, later, all walked on the moon. These men were there to be trained to fly helicopters at Whiting Field. The flight controls on the lunar excursion module that would touch down on the moon were engineered to mimic the controls of a helicopter, although they were controlling thrusters instead of rotor blades. So the choppers were part of the training for those astronauts.

On the very first day of flight school the instructor was giving our class an aviation orientation lecture, and he began by writing two words on the board with a piece of chalk. ALTITUDE/AIRSPEED! *"Gentlemen,"* the instructor began, *"in aviation, you have but two friends. Let's learn this before anything else,"* he said, pointing to the two words. *"These are your insurance policies. The best way for you to get killed in an airplane is to be low and slow."* It was great comedy to me that the last advice I heard from my clueless mother, and the very first advice given to me in flight school were exactly opposite. I did not relate that story to the two astronauts sitting beside me.

All the pilots knew there was a one hundred percent chance that we would all be sent to Vietnam. The only question is whether it was low and slow in a helicopter or high and fast in a fixed wing jet. Guess which one was waiting for me? Mama nailed it again.

Part III -
The Boomer
<u>Generation</u>

Tykie

An individual's self concept is the core of his personality.
    Joyce Brothers

When I was away at college, Mama had only her three youngest to deal with. My younger brother, Tykie, was the oldest and the ringleader. He was born two years after me on September 25, 1943 and was given the name Paschal by his father. One of Pete's friends had a milk plant in Columbia, Tennessee. His friend's last name was Paschal. Tykie didn't let the fact that he had no middle name bother him in the least; in fact, he didn't even know his name was Paschal for a long time. His name was so unusual he didn't even need a last name. Everybody knew him as Tykie, the same way they knew Elvis was Elvis.

And, like Elvis, Tykie was a twin at birth, and his twin brother did not survive. Tykie was smaller than normal when he was born, having had to share the available prenatal space. Someone who saw him as a baby referred to him as a *"little tyke."* This name stuck, and we called him Tykie for the rest of his life.

This youngest set of three children will be referred to as the Boomer Generation, because they were so close to that Boomer phenomenon. Our mother enjoyed a much closer relationship with these three because the nest was much emptier and she had them all to herself. It was fitting that Tykie would be named by his dad, because he took his father's charisma and dramatically improved on it. Tykie was a charmer right out of the chute, and could entertain for hours with his antics. He was small in stature, but when he was in the room his personality was large and in charge. He was never big enough for the odds to favor him in sports, but he could hold his own in just about any situation. To him, life was a play, and games served a social purpose, intended to bring people together. He somehow knew at a very early age that life and people were to be enjoyed to the fullest. We all loved Tykie, and the public shared our enthusiasm. He was our family ambassador and biggest cheerleader. He had a motto to never say anything bad about anybody because it was a small world. Like the proverb says, *"A harsh word, like a stone let go, cannot be recalled."* This trait alone would have made him a popular person.

One of my favorite stories about Tykie happened when he was about six years old. If he woke up early before everybody else, he might walk over to a neighbor's house to find somebody to talk to. This is what happened one Sunday morning that caused a neighborhood panic, and ended with some high drama.

The story started late on a Saturday night in mid July with 18 year old Martha in the bathtub. She heard a tremendous crash, like an earthquake had swallowed a huge tree, or maybe a small plane had fallen from the sky and landed in the back yard. She jumped out of the tub, thinking she might be the next to go, because it sounded like it was two or three feet away from her. It was actually closer than that. A covered well on the other side of the wall, which was sealed off with a slab of concrete, with about six inches of dirt and grass growing over the top of it, had collapsed and imploded into itself, falling some 30 feet below the ground. This was an extremely dangerous situation which none of us even knew existed. There was a faucet directly above the well that someone had left dripping, and the ground was completely saturated. The heavy wet sod and the rotted wood framing of the concrete slab had taken enough abuse. The warranty had expired. The top of the well finally caved in. It could have taken Martha's tub into the hole with it. Instead, she ran out of the bathroom, threw some clothes on, and tentatively peeked out the back door to try to see what aliens really looked like. Seeing nothing in the dark, and afraid to investigate further, she went to bed with half a bath, puzzled and shaken, with absolutely no clue as to what had just happened.

Early the next morning, in daylight, we awoke to much commotion. One of the Hardaway boys next door had discovered the cavernous opening at the corner of our house. The entire neighborhood was soon gathered in awe of this incredibly huge hole in our backyard. The excitement was all fun and games until someone said, "Where's Tykie?" After a short search, Tykie was nowhere to be found. All roads led us back to the hole in the ground, where the gruesome conclusion was suddenly revealed to all of us at the exact same moment. "*Tykie fell into the well.*" In an instant, and quite simultaneously, everybody grew feathers, ran in circles, and turned into a gaggle of Chicken Littles. "*Tykie fell into the well. Tykie fell into the well.*" The word went out, throughout the neighborhood, and even beyond. Within minutes an even larger crowd of rubberneckers had assembled, at least two deep, to stare helplessly down into the black hole that had sucked in Tykie, and God only knows what, or who else. Mama was beside herself, knowing that if Tykie *was* down there in the center of the earth, and not responding to our calls, the news could not be good. All logic was abandoned. Panic replaced reason. The police were called, and they were there in two minutes. The Hardaway kid had already devised a plan to tie a rope around himself, and then have himself lowered down into the well to pull

Tykie out. The police arrived and the Hardaway kid showed up with the rope at about the same time. While everybody was trying to brief the policemen, all at once, and Hardaway was tying himself up and trying to remember the appropriate Boy Scout knot, through all this commotion we heard a small voice from behind us say, "*Gollee!* What's going on?" Tykie had casually walked up behind this cackling herd without being noticed, and completed the modern day parable of having risen from the well. He magically appeared from nowhere. It was biblical.

Joyous shouts of glee exploded from everyone except Hardaway, who was very disappointed for not being the hero and getting his picture in the paper with the rope tied around him. The cops must have thought we were completely insane. The two uniformed policemen just looked at each other, as if to say, "*This calls for a Krispy Krème,*" and got back into their patrol car while the rest of us celebrated Tykie's apparent resurrection. With all the excitement, we didn't even have to go to church that day. We'd had our own Sunday *Miracle on Lincoln Street.* Mama had to go lie down.

When Tykie was about seven years old he charmed a baby squirrel into eating out of his hand and even letting him pick it up. Tykie thought that he and the squirrel were meant to be, so he made a little box for it and brought it into the house. We were all intrigued with the little rodent at first, but as it started to get bigger the amusement wore off for Mama. She didn't want to break Tykie's little heart, because he was so attached to his pet squirrel, but she also didn't want the darn thing running around the house and biting somebody, which it eventually did. It wasn't a big bite, but when some gossipy neighbor told Mama that those things can carry rabies, that was the day the squirrel got the pink slip. But instead of ordering him directly to get rid of the squirrel, she devised a plan for each one of us to convince Tykie that the squirrel had a nice family, and that its mother was worried about it. Besides, squirrels needed to live in the trees to be happy, not in a cardboard box. This plan was working, as Tykie hadn't thought about all that, and he started feeling guilty. Finally, in a real "Opie" moment, Tykie let the squirrel go free, and it never looked back. Later, Mama told Tykie that she thought she saw the squirrel with its mother, and they both looked happy. Everybody bragged on Tykie for being so grown up. We were the ultimate Goobers.

MORRIS KING

Every village has one: an eccentric man who hears his own music. We had Morris King, and he lived across the street from us, about a block away. He was beyond eccentric, and we thought he was one taco short of a fiesta platter. Mama forbade us to say anything bad about him, or anybody else for that matter, and said he was probably shell shocked in the War, whatever that means. He got some sort of monthly check from the government. He had a sister named Venus, but he chose not to stay in the house with her. He lived behind her house in a little shed he had built, just big enough for a small bed and lots of pictures of half naked women that served as wallpaper.

Besides calendar pin-ups, Morris liked bicycles, and would ride back and forth in front of our house with his shirt off whenever my teenage sisters would be in the yard sunbathing. There was plenty of room in the back yard for sunbathing, but the girls spread their blankets out in the front yard in full view of the traffic, so go figure. Morris was harmless really, more of a social deviant than the other kind. He just had a bolt or two that needed to be tightened, and I don't mean on his bike. In spite of all that, he worked on our bicycles and was pretty good at it. He kept most of the kids in the neighborhood in wheels and we tolerated his odd behavior because his mechanical skills were very useful to us, and we were shamelessly selfish, like most kids. I think he felt like the bicycle kids in the neighborhood were his connection to the real world.

He watched all of us grow up, while he fixed our bicycles on a regular basis. We were about the only "friends" he had in terms of regular visitors, and we kept an eye on him as well as having a sneak-peek at his naked pin-ups. Mother always sent him a dinner for Thanksgiving and for Christmas, because she thought nobody else was paying any attention to him. Maybe she liked knowing that there was somebody else out there worse off than we were.

After Ann and Martha won those beauty contests, Morris ramped up his eccentricity to a new level and starting erecting large signs that faced our house extolling the girl's achievements. Maybe he thought he was honoring them, but all it did was embarrass the daylights out of them. There was no rhyme or reason to his odd, billboard sized messages, and in today's litigious society people would lock him up and thrown away the key. But in the Mayberry-RFD world we lived in, Morris King was just another character in the dysfunctional kaleidoscope of comedy that made our simple lives so colorful and hilarious. He was like Floyd the barber on a bicycle. Floyd may have been a little bit shell shocked himself.

Mama's brothers opened a grocery store close to their mother's house in Shelbyville. When the boys closed the store sometime in the mid

Fifties, they had to sell some of their equipment in an auction. After the dust settled, there was one little surprise that Mamas' brothers had put back for a special purpose. I was not at home when they delivered this wonderful secret, but we were all amazed when we came home one afternoon to discover that we were the proud owners of a vintage, electric pin ball machine, complete with a nickel slot. The only space we had to put this monstrosity in our crowded house was in the corner of the kitchen. Sitting right smack in the middle of where most normal people might have had a refrigerator or some useful kitchen appliance, we had a pin ball machine. The poster picture for white trash!

Five shiny steel balls for a nickel complete with flippers and a TILT mechanism! The key was still hanging in the little front door where the nickels collected. There was an instant, ad hoc, pin ball committee to determine the playing protocol and possible ways to profit from this windfall by charging our friends to play. Every kid in the neighborhood was gathered in the kitchen waiting their turn. That machine aged five years on the first day alone. The clamor of ding dongs and click clacks, the cheering and hollering of *I'm next*," and the comings and goings of all these kids who would enter without knocking (we were apparently a commercial enterprise now) would have driven an ordinary woman insane. Mother never complained. To her it was good, clean, harmless fun, and she could keep an eye on us while learning more about the other kids and how we interacted with them.

Our plan to make money from this apparatus lasted about an hour. By then, we had taken the slot door off completely and done away with the pay-for-play plan, mainly because nobody had any money. It was a free for all. Within a week, we had removed the tilt mechanism because it was a nuisance, and one of the little ones had climbed up on the glass top, and cracked it. We removed the glass top altogether because that crack didn't look good, and we could then manipulate the balls by hand, or interfere with one of our competitors for added entertainment. It took about two weeks to lick the red off that candy. Within a month we had reduced that machine to a useless piece of junk, but boy was that fun. As I got older, I saw people pouring money into those pin ball machines, but I had been cured. The bright lights of Vegas had lost their lure. If you've seen one shiny steel ball, you've seen 'em all.

Our holiday visits to Shelbyville to see the Drydens were almost always at Granny Dryden's house. During the summer, there might be an occasional family reunion on the Duck River. Those afternoon picnics on the Duck provided great memories for the little ones. They were mostly hosted by my mother's three brothers who took great pride in making them special for the kids. One of my uncles' friends had a cabin on the river bank with a big back yard full of wooden picnic tables. These picnic reunions were typical pot luck affairs with lots of fried chicken, potato salad and all the Sunday Southern specialties. There were tubs of ice cold watermelon and soft drinks that invited a contest to see which kid could drink the most Nugrape or Orange Crush soda pops. My two look-alike little brothers always stole the show. The uncles joked that they resembled thermometers as they gradually filled themselves up with grape soda that dribbled all over their bare tummies. We had the run of the place and explored that little cabin from top to bottom. They always took a picture on the wooden back steps of Mama and her brood, and that was the highlight of the Sunday. It was always on Sunday after church, a great Southern custom. We were disappointed when the adults started cleaning up the place, because that meant it was time to load up the car and go home. One more Nugrape for the road!

The kids spent a good bit of time at those picnics avoiding Mama's old-maid younger sister Virginia, the schoolteacher, who dispensed guilt like a Pez machine. We knew whatever she had to say to us wasn't going to be something we wanted to hear. We called our Aunt Virginia by the nickname, "Turner," for some reason, and I can't find anybody who knows why. Being sisters, she and my mother were very close, but total opposites as far as I could tell. Turner was a peculiar person with a "hope chest," an odd thing for a grown woman, I thought. I don't know if she ever had a date with a man. She had a puritanical, judgmental nature that made you feel like you were one of her first graders, and I'm sure that didn't help her social life. It also didn't help that she was pear shaped like Ralphie's school teacher in the movie *A Christmas Story*. She did have a big crush on her doctor, a man I only heard of as Dr. Alley. The doctor had performed a surgical procedure on her face and must have possessed a compelling bedside manner. She invited the handsome doctor to go to the annual Tennessee Walking Horse Celebration in Shelbyville, and he accepted. What she wasn't prepared for was for the doctor to bring a beautiful young lady along with him as his date. The teacher had not done her homework on that one. Those horses weren't the only ones sore that night. She changed doctors after that, and never spoke to the man again. Hell hath no fury like a woman scorned.

Tullahoma and Shelbyville are about 15 miles apart, and my family did not have access to an automobile for years. Mamas' brothers had to take turns driving over from Shelbyville to Tullahoma to pick us up and, of course, someone would have to drive us home afterwards. It must have been a real pain in the neck to draw the short straw on that assignment, but they pretended to enjoy it as much as we did. My mother never enforced strict rules on us at home and I think she was happiest when we were all just being ourselves. But on these family get-togethers we all had to suddenly develop our "Sunday School" manners. Like most road trips, it was fun to go to Shelbyville but it was a lot more fun for me when we got back home. When we scrambled out of the car, we all sang the same little four-word song, *"Thanks for the ride,"* followed by three slamming doors. As I got to be a teenager, I usually found excuses not to make those trips, and Mother didn't question my decisions. If I had it to do all over again, as I got older I would have made those visits a higher priority as I got older. They went to a lot of trouble for us. It would be a perfect world if we could live our entire lives without regrets.

Like most youngsters, the basic cause of my discomfort was the excessive amount of sitting around and talking. Nobody seemed to be talking about anything interesting, just nonsense. I got antsy for some action after about an hour. None of the Drydens seemed to know the first thing about sports. They did listen to the World Series (Granny was a Red Sox fan) but didn't talk about sports or play them. They sat in the house and amused themselves by laughing at the little ones. I had three younger siblings, so there were plenty of others to laugh at, but frankly, when I was a youngster I didn't appreciate adults laughing at me. When they weren't talking about nothing, sometimes they would play cards. The favorite card game seemed to be Rook, and the men would mostly play together. If the kids wanted to play cards, "Turner" had a deck of Old Maid cards that she kept in a bookcase. She never saw the irony of having that card deck. When everybody was occupied, it gave me an opportunity to roam from room to room and observe the personalities of these interesting people. The schoolteacher always had a little lesson for each of us. Once she said to me, *"It's not how you give a gift, but how you receive a gift that reveals the kind of person you really are."* Yeah... whatever! Either way I didn't get a gift. They were good people, the salt of the earth. They couldn't help that they were boring.

Mama's three brothers came to these occasions without fail. They were all three extremely loyal, especially to their mother. Our uncle Howard was a War hero who had won the Silver Star in combat. He had an Army surplus Jeep for years, and we would go sit in it when we got bored. He didn't even care if we started it up and went back and forth in the driveway. He left the keys in it all the time. If any adult protested he had an answer, *"Awww... you can't hurt a Jeep."*

Granny would leave cookies and teacakes around so the kids could get to them if the meal was a little late getting started, which it always was. Except for iced tea and coffee, if there was any drinking going on it was just a little nip in the eggnog. I don't think any of those Dryden women ever touched a drop of alcohol.

One year, Howard hosted the Dryden Christmas gathering at his farmhouse in the country just outside Shelbyville. They drew their water from a well that was full of sulfur. It tasted like rotten eggs. You could hardly hold it under your nose without gagging. Of course, they made their iced tea and coffee with it and there wasn't a Nugape in the house. They claimed that the water was healthy, but frankly it made me appreciate the water we drank at home from an old garden hose.

The chaos of gift-giving at Christmas time was burdensome and confusing. There were so many Willis kids that it was finally decided that we should simplify the process with the time-honored tradition of drawing names. One year, when we were visiting the Drydens in Shelbyville, one of my uncles drew Martha's name and got her a salt and pepper shaker. It was a very small box, so he decided to put it into a larger box. He got so carried away with this novelty that when he was finished repeating this box-into-box procedure, the final package was so big it had to be pushed into the room. This corny drama was the climactic highlight of the evening, and amused everyone immensely. (As I said, it was a simpler time.)   After the card games were over and the boiled custard was all gone, my uncle drove us back to Tullahoma with a big salt-and-pepper-shaker grin on his face, and the little ones were asleep before the car got warmed up. If there were any visions of sugarplums, I didn't ever see any.

Growth Of AEDC

As our government pumped more money into the race for space programs, Tullahoma's AEDC continued to hire engineers and other support people, and the little town began to have a constant influx of new families. It seemed like every couple of weeks a new kid would appear at school that everyone made a fuss over. This new kid would get all the attention until the next one came along, and so forth. Pretty soon it got to be *"old hat"* and unless they looked like movie stars, they just had to fit in like the rest of us townies.

These new people began to have a huge effect on our small town culture. Businesses began to grow and so did automobile traffic. Dogs and cats that used to roam lazily through the streets had to start learning to look both ways or stay on the porch. Mama joked that it was getting so crowded that we might have to move to Estill Springs, a real one horse town about 10 miles away. Linda's adopted stray cat, Precious, became a statistic... flattened like a grilled cheese sandwich about 50 yards from our front door. Mama made the boys go get the cat and dispose of it so Linda wouldn't see the grizzly sight. The cat then joined our daddy in the great big world of things that we don't talk about. It took a couple of weeks for Linda to stop singing, *"Here kitty, kitty, kitty."* But by now, we were well-honed in the art of keeping secrets.

Tykie made a point of making friends with every new school arrival, and became a one man Welcome Wagon. So far as we knew, this wasn't anything anybody told him to do, but he had a way of being comfortable with prince or pauper, and he knew these newcomers needed and appreciated his orientation. Before long, the faculty knew to introduce every new student to Tykie, and he would take it from there.

Tykie, age 7

Horse Sense

Patience and perseverance have a magical effect
before which difficulties and obstacles vanish.
  John Q. Adams

Like most parents, my mother had certain idioms and phrases that had become fossilized in her language (see quotes), and we generally knew what she meant by them. Things like *"Don't fall off your high horse"* was similar to *"Don't get too big for your britches"* but not exactly the same, because if you had climbed up on a high horse, you had already gone too far. We never knew where she got that sixth sense that told her that danger was just around the corner.

When Tykie announced that he was going for a horseback ride with an adventurous friend, her comment was predictable, *"You better be careful, those horses don't have a lick of sense."* As it turned out, the horse had more sense than Tykie, because he was the one whose arm was broken when the horse ran under a tree limb and *"knocked him for a loop."* Our good and faithful country doctor, who may as well have been part of the family because he never charged us *"one red cent"* for as long as he treated any of us, did the best he could in resetting Tykie's arm without operating. The break was too severe for a closed reduction, and the arm didn't heal well enough for him to have complete rotation. So much for socialized medicine! Tykie didn't give this *"two thoughts,"* but it was totally unacceptable to our mother. She knew that Sara was over there at nursing school working with some of the best doctors in the world, and she pestered Sara to come up with a solution.

When the time was right, Sara brought Tykie to see the orthopedic specialist that treated the Vanderbilt football team, and Tykie was a big hit instantly. The arm wasn't acceptable to Dr. "Pinky" Lipscome either, so he arranged for it to be fixed properly. Sara got the OK from the head nun at St. Thomas Hospital for Tykie to have a hospital room for his recovery. Tykie had a big celebrity room at the end of the hall, and when the staff heard that Sara had a little brother with a broken arm, they showered him with special attention. Tykie had the night orderly playing cards with him and bringing him extra cookies and ice cream. Nobody wanted Tykie to go home, including Tykie. He had gone from the outhouse to the proverbial penthouse thanks to Mama's persistence and Sara's credibility, and had also become the St. Thomas Hospital mascot. His arm was perfectly normal after that. There surely were many others to thank for that stroke of serendipity, because Mother was braced for a humongous medical bill for all that. But no bill ever came.

True to form, and to the closed communication that existed in Mother's household, nothing was ever discussed regarding Tykie's stillborn twin brother. The hospital in Shelbyville, where he was born, "took care" of the details with as little fanfare as possible, as was the custom in those days. Tykie was a teenager before he ever knew of it himself. But if he couldn't have a twin, he had the next best thing. His little brother, Beau (James Dryden), was born just 15 months after he was, on January 2, 1945. Within a short time the two boys were about the same size, and were often mistaken for twins. It was difficult to say one name without saying the other, like Batman and Robin. Completely different in their personalities, they were almost always together, and the tight bond between them was never broken. They rarely had cross words, got the lion's share of attention wherever they went, and wore the same size clothes.

As close as they were and as similar in size, each had his own unique brand. Beau had the fair skin, blond hair and the reserved personality of the typical Dryden. And he was appropriately named for them, James Dryden. Tykie's face was smothered in his trademark red freckles with an infectious smile that welcomed mischief; a typical no-middle-name Willis.

Part of the harmony between these two can be attributed to the actions of their mother in controlling obnoxious behavior, something she simply would not tolerate. The proximity of their age and size dictated inevitable arguments and shoving matches. Mother despised conflict, and early on when this occurred, she had a very effective solution. She simply locked them in a room and told them to fight until they were sick of fighting. When they begged to stop, Mother told them they didn't look sick enough and closed the door. When the match finally ended, Beau and Tykie never had another serious fight. This story was hilarious to all of us for years, and prompted a follow up round of laughter when they received boxing gloves for Christmas that year. Beau apparently had a silent fury when provoked, but the sickening sight of blood trickling from Tykie's face proved to be a defining moment that terminated his short-lived fighting career. Thus endeth the lesson

Christmas Fire

Either this wallpaper goes or I do.
Oscar Wilde's alleged last words on his death bed.

Beau did his best to burn the house down one Christmas Eve playing with candles. We only saw candles at Christmastime, so we associated Christmas with candles... and candles with fire. Part of the fun, and magic, was playing in all that fire. A match is a magical thing, and as small as it is, it is capable of making very big magic. To tell a kid not to play with matches is like giving him a marshmallow and then telling him not to put it in his mouth. If they didn't want kids playing with matches they should have charged money for them. Matches were free, in little packs of twenty. Christmas was all about fire: fireworks, Yule logs, chestnuts roasting, and flaming candles in the windows. A very dangerous time for kids, really! We even ended the holiday with a big blaze by dragging our dead, dry Christmas tree carcass out in the back yard and striking a match to it. The tree went up like flash paper. Bottom line; Christmas is a great time for kids to play with fire.

Back to the candles, every kid knows that you can drip candle wax all over your hand and make a complete hand mold, never mind the complete mess. On this particular Christmas Eve, Beau had retreated into the living room alone to play with the candle in the front window. You know that window, the one with the cheap little lace curtain that may as well have been coated with gunpowder? That's the one! I walked by just in time so see it happen. The flame never actually touched the curtain, it just had to be close enough to get it warm, and the flames climbed up that wall to the ceiling like a Tabasco'd cat. Instantly, I knew that we could all get out alive, at least I knew I could, but I wasn't sure we could save the house or the presents, which hadn't been opened yet. As soon as I screamed, everyone ran from the kitchen to see what was up. Without blinking, Horace instantly reached into the burning curtain and yanked it to the floor, and every available adult did a flamingo dance on it. Brilliant! The fire was out, problem solved. Any man who handles molten lead for a living isn't going to shrink from a little flaming lace curtain. Two more seconds and the wallpaper above that window would have exploded. We swept up the curtain ashes and looked around for Beau, who was nowhere to be seen. Probably changing his shorts!

We all gathered in the living room to open the presents and all was forgiven. Stuff happens, you know. Beau swallowed the marshmallow. Mama said those old curtains needed to go anyway, she just didn't know they would die so spectacularly. She blamed herself for not taking them down a long time ago. If we heard it once we heard it a thousand times, *"No sense crying over spilled milk."* While we opened the presents, she made sure that Beau sat next to her on the sofa, so everyone could see that there were no hard feelings about the flash curtains. Horace acted as if nothing had ever happened. My mind was racing with "what ifs," as though I would one day be called on to write that story. Later, we shot fireworks.

We always had an old-fashioned, cedar Christmas tree, the free kind that you cut from someone else's property out in the woods. The only kind we could afford. We didn't have it in a container that would hold water to help keep it from getting dry; we just nailed it to a couple of boards with a handful of nails. Within three days it was dryer than the Mohave Desert, but we kept it up for a month. We might as well have had an open keg of dynamite sitting in the corner. By the time we took it down, and dragged it to the front yard, there weren't half a dozen needles left on it. Most of these little needles were hiding in the house somewhere. We didn't own a vacuum cleaner. After Christmas we picked those pesky cedar needles out of every nook and cranny in the house until Easter Sunday. You might even be romping barefoot in May, and step on one. The first warm, sunny day of spring, we took everything out of the house to air it out for spring cleaning, especially blankets and mattresses. Then, we lit another big fire, which we called a bonfire, because it was big and burned everything that we had completely destroyed during the long winter. No burning permit, we just built a big fire, the higher the better. After all, we did get some new stuff for Christmas.

BEAU

Tykie was constantly in physical motion, while Beau was far more deliberate with his energy. During many a barefoot summer, Beau was the ultimate sidekick for Tykie but he insisted on being his own little man. His hair was long, blond and curly and was the envy of all of the girls, and he never liked to have his locks cut off completely, probably for that reason. Given this introduction to these two, it would have been difficult to guess that sports would have come so easily for Tykie's shy little brother. But Beau was indeed an athlete, and established himself at the very first opportunity. And like his older brother Buddy, sports would prove the vehicle in which he would gain some much needed confidence and self-assurance. During one of his first games as a little league baseball player, Beau had an experience that most baseball players never experience in an entire career, a grand slam home run. Ironically, the game was canceled in the very next inning because of rain. The game didn't count for the record, and neither did the home run, but the people who saw it happen, or heard about it, could not disregard the performance. Tykie also played Little League baseball, and was a pretty good shortstop, but he seemed just as happy if his friends on the other team had a good game.

Beau was lucky enough to have a mentor and great coach in junior high school named Milner Carden. Coach Carden came from a large family with a house full of brothers and sisters and could relate to all the Willises. According to Beau, *"He knew how to make a team by using the individual talents of each member of the team. If you weren't very big but had a great arm, the coach would find a way to work you into his plan."* Beau was small, fast, and had a very accurate throwing arm for football. Coach Carden loved to tell the opposing team that his first play from scrimmage was going to be a pass from Willis to Gray for a touchdown. Then he would call that exact play. His players thought he was crazy at first, but after this worked a few times, they thought the coach was some sort of weird football scientist, and they had enormous confidence in him. Beau had watched enough football to understand the game and was several steps ahead of the average player before the game ever started. He had followed my football career, and he knew the Tullahoma High playbook by heart. The high school coaches had all heard of some of Carden's successes and would come to his games to see for themselves. They were salivating at the thought of getting Beau to play for them in high school. Carden was encouraging all this, knowing that Beau would be a good prospect. After all, those same junior high school kids would be growing up together and be even better in high school.

But they forgot one small detail. They forgot to check to see what Beau wanted. Beau had no interest in sacrificing his 115 pound body for the game of football. He could find just as much pleasure and a lot less pain in the game of basketball. The football coaches convinced him that they would not use him as a blocking dummy, and Beau reluctantly gave in to them on the condition that they would use him for his skills, and not for what they hoped he would grow into. As soon as he took to the practice field, however, he became just like everybody else, and lined up against the 200-pounders for dummy practice, just like he knew would happen. As soon as basketball practice started, Beau cleaned out his football locker and turned in his uniform to join the basketball team. This didn't sit well with the coaches, who told him in no uncertain terms that this was not the way things were done. Apparently, if the coaches decided that you were to play football, then by damn, you had to play football. Switching to basketball was not an option and would not be allowed. The old intimidation strategy!

Remember that part where I told you that Beau had a mind of his own? Well, he played his trump card with the coaches when he said, *"That's fine, I can live without either one of them. Thanks for helping me make up my mind."* His plan was to work and earn some money for college, and he was prepared to live with that decision. As soon as everybody regained their senses, Beau was allowed to play basketball and became one of the best point guards that Tullahoma High ever had, winning the coveted J.W. Keller award for leadership on and off the court. Like most small guards coming from small towns, his size and the level of competition made him a long shot for college ball, which didn't happen. Like the rest of the Willis children, Beau needed to earn his own money. With a lot of persistence, Beau worked several hours every week at Weddington Brothers Hardware store. The store was a hangout for middle aged, blue-collar sport's groupies, and had everything but a pot bellied stove. In a small town like Tullahoma, high school sports are a hot topic and Murrell Weddington was a fan of the Willis family and athletics. Beau had a steady, part-time job there for several years and was a popular employee.

When he was a sophomore in high school, he ran for and was elected Vice President of the Student Council for the next year. The upper classman who was elected as President developed a serious illness and was unable to serve his term. As Vice President, Beau then filled the vacancy and served as President during his junior year, a job normally held by a senior. During the end of his term, when it was time to run for re-election, Beau did not feel that he should enter the race for President since he had not actually been elected to that position and had been "given" the honor by an unfortunate circumstance. Some of his teachers advised him to run anyway, but he stuck to his guns. His good friend Jim Phillips ran away with the election and Beau enjoyed that result more than holding that office for another year.

We can only see what we are prepared to see.
  unknown

During Beau's senior year at Tullahoma High, the school had a Career Day. This was a time when you were given a half day off from school and the opportunity to contemplate your life after graduation. Then you were to come back and report on your vision of your future. Most of the students went to the drug store or the pool room, but Beau had a goal to become an optometrist, so he made an appointment to see Dr. Barber, a thriving young optometrist in Tullahoma.

The doctor took Beau under his wing, and promised to sponsor his "vision" by loaning him the money for college, and then hiring him as an apprentice partner after college. Beau would receive an interest free loan from the doctor, which he could repay from his wages over time. This was more than Beau could have imagined, and he was ecstatic to have his dream plan so well constructed and organized. No records of these conversations were kept, and the good faith arrangement ended suddenly when the young doctor passed away less than two years later, of a heart attack. Beau was torn between the loss of his friend, and the loss of his career arrangement, but he was in no position to approach the doctor's widow for answers about their arrangement. Beau's tale of woe was the last thing she needed to hear. There was supposed to have been an insurance policy that guaranteed the arrangement. Beau checked on this with the doctor's insurance agent and got a predictable response. *"Huh?"*

The doctor's wife would later teach classes at the same college that Beau attended.

***

Pioneering The World's First Turbine Powered Helicopter

Nothing illustrates opportunity in America more than the story of how I got into the securities business. It all started on a rainy day. I was stationed in Jacksonville, North Carolina right out of flight school, preparing to be sent to Vietnam. North Carolina had its share of rain, which would be good training for the monsoons of Southeast Asia. One morning when the planes were grounded because of bad weather, all the officers assembled in the ready room for a leadership meeting. The Commanding Officer of our squadron decided to call on one of the pilots to give a spontaneous leadership talk for three or four minutes. Being a new guy, I got the random nod. I had the 10 steps between my seat and the podium to think of something compelling to say.

On the way up to the front of the room, I saw a picture of the Huey helicopter that we were all flying. Underneath the picture of the chopper were the words, "Pioneering the world's first turbine powered helicopter." There was no microphone, so when I got up to the hot spot, I cleared my throat and began by saying those exact words in a loud but uncertain voice. I was shooting in the dark. After a long, pregnant pause, I added, *"Do you all realize what we are actually doing here?"* Another dramatic pause! *"We are all pioneers."*

From there, I went on to say that in the future there would be choppers flying medevac missions up and down the interstates of America, and saving the lives of traffic casualties by rushing them to hospital pads all across the country, just as we were training to do in combat. Because of the work we were doing, I "envisioned" choppers hauling prefab condos to mountain resorts and other remote areas in support of the construction industry. The officers were settling into my speech now.

"Because of us," I went on, *"commercial applications for helicopters in the future would be enormous, and we, as innovators of this phenomenon, had bright futures waiting for us in the business world. This was a new area of opportunity, and we were the risk takers that were making things happen. These opportunities were being made possible because of the work that we were doing as pioneers of the world's first turbine powered helicopter. What a terrific investment opportunity this was, and it was all right under our noses. Why then, were we not buying Textron stock, the parent company of Bell Helicopter, who would have to make thousands of helicopters to supply the demand?"*

I was on a roll. By the time the five minute BS session was over, they were whipped into a froth. My imagination was so active that I had beads of sweat forming on top of my head. Several of the men left the room immediately and called their brokers, including the Commanding Officer.

In the next several months Textron nearly tripled. I have no idea why. This was 1965.

From that point on, I was the go-to-guy for investment advice for the entire base. When the word got out that there was a stock market guru and clairvoyant in their midst, I was sought out for my opinion on everything from the Manhattan Fund to Mobile Oil. I wouldn't have touched Textron with a 10-foot pole, because, of course, I had invented all this in my head out of sheer desperation for a five minute leadership exercise. But some of the senior officers, and several of my friends, bought in to my fairy tale and purchased the stock. I didn't know the first thing about Textron, and didn't even have a broker. But I also didn't try to stop anyone from buying it either. There are no victims, only volunteers, I thought. They were big boys, and none of them were strangers to risk taking. Had the stock gone the other way, I might have stayed a 2nd Lieutenant for a long time.

With this speech, I had set a new standard for those leadership classes, and all the officers began working on their speeches for the next rainy day. But I don't think we ever did that again, so they all gave their dramatic speeches anyway, around the coffee pot, trying to top mine. The whole culture had changed. All those investment queries forced me to spend some time researching the answers to all the questions I was getting.

I was spending a little spare time calling stockbrokers, and getting copies of Standard and Poor's reports, which I brought back to the ready room. A star was born.

On a visit to a brokerage office to get some information, the manager asked me what I was going to do when I got out of the service, and he suggested I might do well as a stockbroker. I was given lengthy academic and psychological testing to determine if my ice cream and my *"wanna buy a paper"* selling skills had prepared me for selling sophisticated investment products. It turned out that they were eerily compatible. I was accepted immediately. This launched a 34-year career for me in the business of finding out what investment flavors people liked and getting it for them. I had read somewhere that if you help enough people get what they want; you can eventually get everything you want.

I was never sure why intelligent adults thought that any broker would know if a stock would go up or down. It seems to me that if anyone had that information, just one time, it would be enough to be set for life. But to presume to know on a daily basis seems ludicrous. Nevertheless, even the rookie brokers spoke with supreme confidence about things they knew less that nothing about. But like the Textron stock, the market kept going higher, and the process held its charm for both brokers and clients alike, sometimes with amazingly positive results. We are all ignorant, but on different subjects.

Boo Radley

Men in general, especially athletes and pilots, like to give each other nicknames. It's a convoluted, macho way of showing mutual respect with an added layer of sarcastic disparagement. Outside of a football locker room, a ready room full of Marine pilots is about as thick as testosterone is likely to get. You are nobody until you get a nickname, and you never know when or how your new name will materialize. In Vietnam, I was labeled Boo Radley. As pilots, we spent 100% of our time together, eating, sleeping, flying, planning and talking. Each pilot was consumed in his own embellished version of his most recent outlandish act of heroism. The conversations could get pretty one-dimensional with little else being discussed other than the last mission, or the next one. Since we were all doing the same kinds of things, I found the exaggerated details of these conversations extremely boring. To shake things up a little, I suggested that we should all read the same books, so we could have something to talk about other than telling exaggerated stories about our combat missions. It was going to be a long tour if all we did was create our own fiction.

Someone sent me a copy of Harper Lee's 1960 classic, *To Kill a Mockingbird*, which I passed around the ready room. The guys fell in love with the book and they fought over who would get it next. Boo Radley's character was one of the mockingbirds in the book, but underlying his goodness was an initial shroud of reclusive creepiness that dominated the imaginations of the kids in the story (and the pilots in the ready room). In the book, Boo eventually comes out of nowhere to rescue the kids when they are threatened by evil, and he emerges the hero. Great book! So… how did the story relate to me?

One day, when I was assigned the 24 hour medevac duty, I was napping on the top bunk in the ready room resting up for the next harrowing "911" call. The others were engrossed in the planning of a mission that involved just about everybody else but me. They apparently did not hear the field phone call in a medevac mission, or see me slip out of the door to the medevac plane. A few minutes later, they heard my voice crackle on the radio. I was already preparing to land in the zone to pick up the casualties. Surprised to hear my voice, they all looked over at the empty bunk where they had seen me sleeping, seemingly "seconds" ago, and one of them remarked. *"He's like Boo Radley. He just shows up out of nowhere."* From that day on, I was Boo, and the name stuck for years. I had to ask why I was Boo, because I missed all that. But it turned out to be a good nickname. It didn't have to make complete sense.

LINDA

*I like the kind of teacher that gives you something to
take home and think about besides homework.*
    Edith Ann

According to Beau, his little sister could read before he could. Linda
loved school and always had an armload of books with her. To say
that she was the teacher's pet might have been an understatement
because; even as a student she was practically a substitute teacher.
Anyone with a keen eye toward the future could have predicted ac-
curately that she was destined to become a teacher.

But somehow, through her vicarious adventures as a voracious reader, another passion awakened in her...the desire to travel. Her cu-
riosity for foreign lands and foreign languages, fed by stories from
her favorite teachers with similar interests, stoked the fire in her.
According to her, *"The two places I always felt safe, secure and happy
were at school and at home. One of my most respected teachers, Mrs.
Blanche McClure, recommended that I focus my studies on computer
sciences because that would be the next big thing. She was right, of
course, but the lure of languages and travel had already taken root, and
I was hooked."*

When Linda started first grade, East Lincoln Elementary School
was just across the street. Walking to school, the little ones were
required to go down to the corner, well past the front door of the
school, where the patrol guards monitored the only supervised crossing. The sixth graders, top dogs of the elementary school, served as
patrol guards. If you crossed anywhere else, and got caught, you

could be in big trouble. Being a patrol guard was the queen mother of all rewards for a sixth grader. For one entire week, two selected kids (boys only, as it seems that it was a gender thing) got to hold those long poles with red flags, and wear yellow vests with badges on them. Those badges created some sort of metamorphosis, and instantly transformed the boys into high ranking Gestapo Generals. The only thing missing was the machine gun. Smiling indicated a lack of seriousness, and was not allowed. Talking was also discouraged. Crossing the street was a very dramatic, life or death situation, and not to be taken lightly, at least during the week that I was a patrol guard. Just try to imagine some kid getting knocked over by a family station wagon and having his underwear examined on your watch.

All this was just part of our overall education which started with our learning to read. Our first school book was Mac and Muff. We all had to read it. It had a total of about 20 words, all arranged in different but similar sentences. Mama wanted her preschoolers to get a head start on reading, so we had to hear this primer a million times. By the time Linda, the youngest, got to first grade, she knew the book by heart. Mac was a dog and Muff was a cat. The book instructed the reader to observe their activities, i.e., See Mac run. See Muff run. A pretty thin plotline to say the least, and the writer never bothered to explain why they were running. We assumed it was because dogs like to chase cats. But, in our neighborhood, we had seen what happens when a dog actually catches a cat, and it was not a pretty sight. Our new first grader, Linda, wondered why chasing cats was so amusing, since she adored cats, and had one of her own at the time, that she named Precious. She also wondered why they never used girl patrol guards. A new generation of independent thinkers was beginning to emerge.

Linda was a precocious child, and being precocious has its challenges. The youngest in a litter of nine can get spoiled with all the attention, and Linda was no exception. She definitely had a squeaky wheel, but it didn't take a village to straighten out a problem when Mama was on top of her game. When the six year old decided she would run away from home if she didn't get her way, Mama helped her pack her things in a shoe box, walked her to the front porch, and wished her well. Tykie and Beau were sent to "keep their distance, but to keep an eye on her." Linda made it about a block and a half before reality kicked in. One positive benefit from growing up in a large family is that foolishness polices itself, so when you make a fool of yourself, you will get kidded about it until you are forced to acknowledge the error, and laugh at yourself. The message was pretty simple. We didn't really have the luxury of high maintenance behavior.

Linda was also studying piano when she was in first grade, but we didn't have a piano, of course. Her lessons basically consisted of learning the keys, and the chords, on a fold out piece of paper that mimicked the keyboard. Learning to play the piano on a paper keyboard is equivalent of learning to play guitar on a broom, but Linda persevered (in spite of handicaps). When Ms. Carol Bean, our perennial first grade teacher, heard about Linda's piano plight, she offered to give Mother a piano for Linda. It was a broken down relic, out of tune, with a couple of keys that didn't even make a noise, but it had to be better than a piece of paper. One day the piano showed up at our house and everybody banged around on it for a few days until the new wore off, and then Linda had it all to herself. After a year or so of lessons, the piano students were expected to perform a recital, to show off their skills. Linda had worked hard on her tune, which was called "Airy Fairies." This was the number she would showcase at her recital, and the number that had driven us all completely nuts for several months. Tykie and Beau were relentless with their mockery of her leading up to her recital. They would sit at the piano and announce that they were now going to play their favorite classic, "Airy Fairies." All this was fun and games until Mama dropped the bomb on them. *"You are all going to attend Linda's recital."*

This was the first of several of those recitals, but it was by far the hardest one to sit through. All the other piano kids and their parents were there, about 20 of them, with Sunday school clothes, of course. Not knowing when her brothers were going to look at each other, and lose it, while Linda pecked her way through that song, occasionally hitting one of those broken keys, was one of the most challenging feats of self control we were ever asked to endure. It didn't help that Mama positioned herself next to Linda, so she could see us, and we could see her own lip start to quiver when she, too, almost lost her composure a couple of times. Linda was nervous, but stoic and determined, and at the end we were very proud of her. The enthusiastic applause at the end was more relief than appreciation, but she didn't have to know that.

Eventually her weekly piano lessons were replaced by basketball and track. She was approached by Beau's favorite coach, Milner Carden, who convinced her that she could do anything that anyone else could do, with the proper application. But whether she was running against her boyfriend for student council president (true story), or running the 440 relay, she was an individual to the core and remained that way.

When it was her time to compete in the Miss Tullahoma Pageant, Linda found a way to inject her own individual style over the advice of her sisters and Mother. Linda was carefully coached and crafted for the big night, from her hairstyle to her high heel shoes. Never mind that 15 year old girls aren't that comfortable in high heels, after all, it was a level playing field for all of them. Nothing was left to chance, as Sara and her mother left Linda backstage to wait her turn for the walk down the runway. But as Linda put it simply, *"They made one little mistake, they left me alone."* It seems that while she was waiting to be introduced, the little red booties that they gave her to wear backstage, felt far more comfortable to her than those cumbersome high heels. And the more she pranced around backstage the more comfortable they became. *"Why not just wear the booties?"* This is exactly what she did, much to the dismay of her coaches and the bewildered judges. The results were predictable from there. Linda would get another chance in another year and would not repeat that gaff again, but there was just something about a beauty contest that was difficult for Linda to take seriously. Over the years, her approach to a beauty contest proved a far more entertaining story than if she had brought home a trophy.

Dale Robertson's Secrets Of Public Speaking

New York City

November 11, 2008, 10:20am

On the day Lee and I were scheduled to be on the NBC show, a 72 foot Christmas tree had been delivered during the night to Rockefeller Plaza. The attention-getter-du-jour was a hot topic. We learned in the TODAY show green room that in 1931 the tree had been used as a Christmas tree by Mary Varanyak, when she was a little girl in New Jersey. After that Christmas, Mary planted the tree in her yard and, as it grew, she predicted for years that it would one day end up in Rockefeller Center. Mary died in 2000 and did not get to see her prediction come true. This is the kind of drama that can only happen in a city like New York, and only in America.

The NBC makeup artist was powdering my forehead and a hair stylist was poking around with Lee's hair as she sat in the chair next to mine. He was making Lee uncomfortable by making subtle changes to her hair style. When he finished, Lee slipped off into a nearby restroom and put it back like it had been before he fiddled with it. Apparently, she was not a tree that needed to be redecorated. We were just toe-tapping and waiting to be called on to the set. Lazar, Freidman and Bellochio had already disappeared, and had gone somewhere to rehearse their secret song.

I was no stranger to public speaking and rarely got nervous unless I was trying too hard to impress. I had learned a good lesson about that back in my days as an office manager when I conducted training for brokers. During one of those training sessions in the home office in Nashville, I was invited to give a talk on how to sell bonds. I did this strictly off the cuff, because I coached the same thing almost daily in my branch, so it wasn't new material. My boss liked my presentation, and he asked me if I would be willing to make a video of the talk to send to all the brokers in the system. I was flattered, and they set up a film crew for seven o'clock the following morning.

That night I couldn't sleep well for wanting this filmed version to win some sort of Emmy award. I woke up every few minutes to add something to my notes. That's right, now I had comprehensive notes. I had no notes before. By 5am I was wired, and decided to get up to practice. I got dressed, and went downstairs for breakfast. There were only two other people at the Hyatt Hotel in downtown Nashville that morning. They were waiting for the hostess to seat them. When I walked up behind them and said good morning, I recognized the two men. Roger Maris (61/61) and Dale Robertson (Death Valley Days) spoke back.

As soon as they were seated, Dale motioned to me and asked if I wanted to join them.

My mind was on my Oscar-winning film presentation, but I wasn't about to pass up a chance to sit with these two superstars. They were there for The Vinnie, an annual charity golf tournament hosted by Vince Gill. I was having trouble understanding why I was nervous over the same speech that I had given so effortlessly the day before. As soon as the attention turned to me, I used the opportunity to ask a question.

I told them about the film, and asked the actor how he was able to control himself in situations like that. Dale answered without hesitation. *"That's an easy one. You're trying to be something you're not. Put all those notes away and just say what you have to say and sit down. You can't read notes, think, act and talk all at the same time. So just talk. Talk like you are doing with us right now."* He told me that Will Rogers gave him some good advice when he was first asked be in movies. Rogers told him not to take acting lessons or change his way of talking. He said that most people liked their grits straight up.

Maris didn't talk very much during that breakfast except when Dale got up to take a phone call. Then he told me that the two of them had been playing together in those charity events for years, and that Dale was a real cowboy. He never read the newspapers and was a very opinionated, far-right-winger. He said that Dale thought the liberals and the media were taking the country straight to hell in a hand basket. Then when Maris got up to go to the men's room, Dale said that it was ironic that I asked him the question I did, because Maris, himself, had always been nervous about talking, especially to the press, *"and now, look at him, he's got throat polyps."* It was interesting that Maris offered me absolutely no advice on public speaking that morning. They were like the Odd Couple.

Since then, I have used Dale's advice about public speaking and it's been a lot easier; no Oscars, but I enjoyed less stress. Now, when I have to speak to an audience I just try to have two or three things to say and keep it simple. Nobody wants a long lecture anyway. I think Dale gave some good advice. *"Be natural."* We are who we are.

Maris died about a year later of throat cancer. He was only 51. Dale was the same guy who did those Pall Mall cigarette commercials, but he had quit smoking by then. Maybe Dale's wisdom would serve me well during my national television interview.

FINAL CHAPTER

When you do nothing, you feel overwhelmed and powerless. But when you are involved, there is the sense of hope and accomplishment that comes from knowing that you are making things better.
   Unknown

In late 1963, while I was flying low and slow in flight school in Pensacola, my sister Sara and Martha's husband, George decided to purchase a brand new home for the purpose of giving Mother a carefree place to live for the rest of her life. This new house, at 609 Hardison Place in Tullahoma, would be headquarters for all the spring breaks, summer vacations, and holiday comings and goings of Mama's pack. Sixteen years had come and gone since she had assumed the duty of parenting nine children without a penny to her name. A glimmer of light was beginning to form at the end of her tunnel. In 1965, she graduated her last baby from Tullahoma High School. Linda was a straight A student and received an academic scholarship to Middle Tennessee State University, about 35 miles away. Tykie was serving a three year tour of duty in the Navy and was stationed aboard the USS Kitty Hawk, an aircraft carrier. Beau was pursuing his optometry studies at Martin College and by then, I was flying airplanes for the Marine Corps in Jacksonville, N.C.

For the previous two years Mama had enjoyed a less hectic parenting role, and was able to enjoy a more intimate and personal relationship with Linda. Comparing pictures of Mother and Linda as adolescents, they looked almost identical, and I think Linda reminded Mama of her own childhood. All of Mother's children wrote letters to her regularly, and phoned her from time to time. She was unusually shy on the phone for some reason, and not very talkative, almost like a little girl who was embarrassed that someone was paying attention to her. I was both amused and puzzled by her diffidence on the phone, because it was difficult to have a phone conversation with her.

The next couple of years should have been some of the more normal and stress-free periods of her adult life. Her penchant for looking to the future proved prophetic, as Sara, the nurse, would be her close companion and confidant so that she was never completely alone.

An Avon saleslady called on Mother and convinced her to offer cosmetic products to her neighbors and her friends. There was no investment or risk, so she decided to give it a try. It was more of a hobby than a job for her, and it took her back to her younger, unmarried days of being an office manager for a food broker. She needed to feel productive, and her cubs had dispersed into the world. She could handle this. She used to tell the story on herself in her youth as a food broker that a customer had rudely challenged her quote on a case of eggs by saying that the newspaper had advertised them cheaper than she had quoted them. She was only 22 years old at the time, and her boss may not have been completely pleased with her response when she advised the caller to go ahead and buy them from the newspaper. She normally had a passive personality, but, apparently, in her youth she could hold up her end of a conversation. But this story was in sharp contrast to the timid tone that I was hearing on my long distance phone calls to her.

Something didn't seem quite right about that.

In July of 1966, Sara married David E. Reichenau, an aeronautical engineer who worked at AEDC where she was employed as a nurse. I could only hear about their wedding through the mail. July 1966 was one of the busiest months of my aviation career. My squadron was fully engaged in Operation Hastings in Vietnam. During my 14-month tour in that combat area, Hastings was the biggest strategically coordinated initiative of the war, and I was neck deep in it. Altogether, I logged 642 sorties, or missions, as a pilot in that combat zone, many of them were medevac missions in the UH1E. The "Huey" was the world's first turbine powered helicopter, and we were its pioneer pilots, remember?

Medevac is the most dangerous, but also the most rewarding of all combat missions. Mostly because where you find a wounded soldier, you usually run into the people that wounded him. I wrote hundreds of pages of memoirs about that tour of duty and sent them home as a "round robin" to be passed down a chain so that my entire family would be able to read them. I chose to avoid graphic stories of guts and gore, or the details of my being shot down twice, for obvious reasons. It would have driven my hand wringing Mother over the edge to know what her son was really doing over there. I wrote mostly about the peaceful portion of life in Vietnam, like what we had for dinner, or long descriptions of our living conditions, and how we had to heat our shower water in 55 gallon drums... *I saw a white elephant in the jungle today,* type thing. I didn't see any sense in worrying my family about wounded Marines and flaming helicopters. Ironically, low and slow pretty much described those medevac missions.

Thanks For The Ride

New York City

13 November, 2008 10:30 am

I barely remember being escorted back from the green room to the set of the TODAY Show. We were engrossed in conversation with our escort David when we suddenly appeared in front of the cameras during a long news break. They were discussing the arrival of the 72 foot Christmas tree. We were introduced to Hoda Kotb. They call her Hoda Lee, my wife was Susan Lee, and of course, there was Kathie Lee. I wanted to get some mileage out of that, but the opportunity never came up.

All the performers had resurfaced and were in their place. David Freidman was at the piano, and had co-written the song that I was going to hear for the first time in about 10 minutes. Dave Bellochio sat behind a keyboard synthesizer, which I assumed could imitate a variety of musical sounds. Both these men had changed clothes, and had been through makeup since I last saw them. Aaron Lazar, the best looking man I had ever seen in New York, stood beside the piano with a microphone in his hand. He was dressed in solid blue. Hoda had worn an all-white dress, and her co-host was in a red dress. The red, white and blue theme was probably not a coincidence. I sat on the sofa with the three Lee girls in front of five cameras, all with double monitors. The top screen showed what the viewers were seeing on their TV sets at home, and another teleprompter displayed the scripted part of the show for Hoda and Kathie Lee. I could see BUD AND LEE WILLIS in all caps on the monitor among the other words that I figured were none of my business. Lee and I had no script. I had gone over in my mind many times what they might say to me, but after watching their show a few times in preparation for this, I had no clue as to what might be asked. It was just live TV, when the camera rolls, anything could happen.

The four of us chatted with most of the attention going to Hoda. We had not met her and she seemed to want to catch up with her co-host in getting to know the two new guests. Their relaxed manner, especially Kathie Lee's down home style of girl-next-door banter, put us at ease. Jayme Baron, the producer, was behind the camera moving around from place to place, either nervous about the details of the show, or the uncertainties of live television, or both. This was her baby, and it was do-or-die time. Suddenly, one of the camera crew interrupted and started a countdown beginning at nine seconds. The seconds also appeared on the teleprompter. We had received no instructions except where we would sit. At the count of zero, the two hosts appeared on the monitor and Hoda began speaking the line assigned to her. Kathie Lee then read her line but neither sounded as though they were reading. Both looked straight into one of the cameras. She introduced the story that my wife had encouraged me to send in for the *Everyone Has a Story* series. My face appeared on the screen, and we sat watching the film that I had shot two days before with Jayme.

I looked fatter and older on the screen than I thought I would. The first words out of my mouth may have helped explain some of that, "*In 1966, I was a young Marine aviator, flying Hueys out of Danang.*" Anyone with a quick mind for numbers would have known immediately that I was eligible for Medicare. The rest of the story lasted about three minutes, and my version was chopped down by the producers to about half what I had written and read on the tape. Being a southern boy, I'm not a fast talker, so the editor had to crunch my story to fit the three-minute time space. The background music, and the American flag superimposed behind me on the film, added to the poignancy of the story. This is the full text of what I wrote:

In 1966, I was a young Marine aviator flying Hueys out of Marble Mountain near Danang. My squadron was VMO2. We were supporting the Marines in that area.

One of our top priorities was to get the wounded out of the combat area and into the hospital as quickly as possible. Medevac is the most rewarding of all combat missions but it is also the most dangerous. We knew we were saving lives but we also knew that where you find a wounded Marine, you are likely to find the people that wounded him.

We flew hundreds of these type missions but one stands out above all others. I was called to pick up a casualty and take him to a special facility that treated life or death combat injuries. There was a corpsman, a crew chief and a co-pilot in the plane with me. I had learned early to look straight ahead when picking up the wounded and to keep my mind on the business of flying the chopper. Some of the sights could be overwhelming and I was a young pilot with no medical experience.

This was not always possible, especially on this particular mission. The young Marine was missing a leg, an arm, an eye and an ear. The leg and the arm were wrapped in a poncho that was placed in the plane beside his stretcher. The hospital was 15 minutes away and I had the airspeed redlined while still trying to give the wounded soldier and the corpsman a smooth ride. The corpsman held a plasma bag over his only arm and gave him a shot of morphine in his only leg.

When we landed at the hospital pad, the medical staff rushed to assist with the stretcher. Our crew transferred the man and the poncho to the doctors and prepared to leave the area. Our job was done. But just as they reached the front door of the hospital with the stretcher they stopped, and something extraordinary happened. One of the doctors ran back to our chopper and called the crew chief back. I could see the wounded soldier motion for the crew chief to lean forward so he could tell him something over the noise of the rotor blades.

In a few seconds he was back in the plane and gave me the thumbs up for takeoff.

I could see that tears were streaming from his eyes. It took about a minute for him to gather himself and speak into his mic.

"Captain Willis, do you know what he said to me. He said to tell the pilot, thanks for the ride."

On the way back to the base we were all bawling like babies instead of combat tested Marines. When we landed and shut down I told the others that I prayed to God that young man would live to change as many more lives as he had that day with that simple gesture. Any man who could see through his own incredible circumstances and still have the presence of mind to say thank you, still brings tears to my eyes today, and I can hardly bear the telling of it. I have told this story many times to teary eyed audiences with the message that we should always show gratitude and thank people every day, and to thank God for heroes like that young Marine.

I had not seen the edited film version of my story, and, as many times as I had heard the message, I was still moved by it. Suddenly we were live. Kathie Lee thanked us for being there and I responded by thanking her for letting us honor soldiers everywhere and introduced my beautiful wife Lee. Lee explained why she nagged me into writing the story in the first place and immediately stole the show. Hoda asked how this defining moment had changed me, and I told her it made me want to be more like the young Marine in the story. It was all about the power of gratitude, and the story demonstrated how a simple expression of appreciation can change people. I suggested that if we made a point to say *"thank you"* to at least one person every day that our lives would gradually get better. That was it. It was as simple as that.

Aaron Lazar then sang the song that David Freidman and Kathie Lee had written for the story that had been kept a closely guarded secret. The name of the song is *"Carry Us Through."*

It was just another day, doing what I had to do

War is hell they say, but what they say is true

It was just another day, flying soldiers through the sky

And I learned to look away, so I wouldn't see them die.

At this point I almost lost it. Hearing my own words set to music and sung by this powerful artist penetrated my soul. My eyes were about to burst. The story was hard enough to write in the first place. At 3 am on the morning that I wrote it, I cried so much that I decided to go outside and cry as hard and as long and as loud as I needed to until I was finished. Knowing that I was going to read it aloud in front of a camera, I tried to rehearse it with a stiff upper lip, but was never able to get through it without choking up. I finally decided that I would just have to live with it if it happened on the air. The next verse was even more painful.

It was just another day for me, just more of the same

Pick up another casualty, and never know his name

But this time, I don't know why, I watched them carry him off

He was only just a boy, but half the boy was gone.

My heartbeat had slowed to nothing at this point, and it wasn't from the Metoprolol that I was taking for the four stents the cardiologist had put in my heart last October. I wanted to lie down and put my head in Lee's lap and be very still for awhile.

But Aaron was just getting started.

Carry us through the clouds Lord, carry us through the rain

Carry us through the storms ahead, carry us through the pain.

Everyone in the room had tears in their eyes at this point and the place was perfectly still, mesmerized. The camera alternated shots between Aaron singing and my reaction to the song. I don't know what was gripping me more, the lyrics or his performance. I hoped they had a chopper waiting to medevac *me* when this was over.

It was just another day, when they took him from the plane

He never did cry out, he never did complain

And as they carried him away, he said, just before he died

He said tell the pilot thanks, thanks for the ride.

Carry us through the pain Lord, carry us through the wars

Carry us through the storms ahead; carry us through deaths' doors.

Carry us through, carry us through, carry us through

So we can say, "Thanks," another day.

If poetry is supposed to transcend, it had done a number on me. I was toast. To me, that song was like a prayer of absolution for all the families of all the men and women who ever paid the ultimate sacrifice for our country, especially the mothers who raised them.

I was beyond crying at this point. A handful of talented artists had done something that I never expected. They had personally delivered closure and a message of peace at the same time. I was moved into another dimension and so were a million others. But I wasn't thinking about anyone else when Dave Bellochio played the last note of that song. This moment was for me and that young Marine. With the help of all these talented artists, I had finally thanked the brave man who changed my life 43 years ago.

I stood up and gave them all a standing ovation but looked right into Aarons Lazars' eyes. He knew he had nailed it. As many times as he had rehearsed that song, he didn't really know what he had until he experienced our reaction to it. He was moved as much as anyone at the emotion in the room and the reverence that his performance had resonated. I looked around for Jayme, thinking that they might bring her up on the set.

Two Marines came out and received a check from NBC for the Wounded Warrior Project. They had both sustained combat injuries in Iraq.

We closed the show by presenting each of the performers with one of my air medals that Lee had made into necklaces. We all knew that we had shared a special morning together. Everyone stayed around for a long time taking pictures of each other, talking and laughing.

Jayme and I had the same happy look of relief on our faces. We were glad the play was over.

The show was a terrific hit. For the next half hour, people took pictures of us like we were Brad Pitt and Angelina Jolie. Then we just stood around on the set talking and joking with the staff. Actually, I felt better than Brad Pitt, knowing I didn't have to go home to all those kids. But home we went, because after the show the phone calls and emails was so overwhelming that we could not feel comfortable trying to be normal in that wonderful city for all the contacts that needed our attention. We could always come back to New York, but right now we needed to get back to our comfort zone. For the first time, I had a better understanding of why some of those celebrities take drugs.

Apparently my wife was right when she said that people needed to know and appreciate the fact that there was another war going on, and that this was an especially sensitive time for our nation. A lot of people were under stress. Both the market and the economy were in the tank, and it was time to get back to basics. The simple act of gratitude might be a good place to start.

The media rush lasted for about three weeks, and it was obvious that this live TV show and its message had resonated with a huge audience. I had no idea so many people watched daytime television. Lee and I were astonished by the hundreds of responses, some as poignant as the story itself. We realized that the main reason for the strong reaction was that Jayme and I had kept the story simple. A single point of light! It was all about the power of gratitude and how two simple words have the magic to change a person's life forever: *thank you!*

Jayme knew her show was a winner. The stock market even went up 442 points that day. Back home in Naples we tried to get back to normal, paying bills and handling our day to day affairs, but the phone kept ringing. Talk of a follow up show was in the air. It was hard to focus with people calling and emailing, some that I haven't seen or heard from in 50 years. Requests for radio, newspaper interviews and speaking engagements needed our attention. We were getting addicted to all the personal attention. Being celebrities had fried our brains. It was hard to focus. I needed this to be over. In a few days we got a letter from the IRS questioning a small travel expense from three years ago. I have never been questioned about taxes before, and I couldn't help but wonder if my new found TV notoriety was the cause of it. One thing is certain; nothing can burst your bubble faster than a letter from the IRS. When I finally got my head cleared, I went back to my writing chair, closed the door and began revising the memoir that I had written for and about my family. Now I had a reference for my point of light.

Mama Gets Sick

For the strength of the Pack is the Wolf,
And the strength of the Wolf is the Pack.
    Rudyard Kipling

After Sara was married in July of 1966, my mother experienced something she had not experienced in her entire life. She was alone. Now she had time to think. She even had the luxury of thinking about herself. I still wonder what went through her mind. I wonder if she realized what I was really going through in Vietnam, and how these things were changing me. Television coverage of the war was exactly the opposite of my letters. But she had a way of blocking herself off from the overwhelming complexities of life. I think they call it compartmentalizing, but it seemed like, now, she was disoriented, without the day to day tumult of her kids around. That was her strength, and it had been taken away. For some reason, unknown to anyone, she showed no interest in driving a car or getting a driver's license. She also never bothered to obtain a divorce from her estranged husband, which would have been a simple, legal formality. Even more odd, is that we never asked her why. Now, she was alone, and all she had were the secrets locked inside her. And they stayed that way.

Within two years, Mama was beginning to experience health problems related to her bladder and her kidneys. Nurse Sara spearheaded the effort to get her some medical attention, and they visited a local doctor who shall remain nameless. The doctor told Mama that it was probably her nerves; that she was just bored, and worried because she didn't have her children at home anymore. His advice to her was to go home and stop worrying. Hearing this infuriated Sara, because the doctor had not ordered a single test to confirm his folksy evaluation. Her sister Martha agreed that this was ludicrous, and decided to seek the council of doctors in Huntsville. A series of tests proved this to be a wise decision. She tested positive for cancer of the uterus. Mama was very sick. Some valuable time may have been wasted there, but a series of radiation treatments were begun immediately. The light at the end of her tunnel turned out to be an oncoming train.

Radioactive pellets were inserted into the affected areas to try to reduce the growth of the cancer cells. The pellets basically burned up everything they touched. This procedure was repeated several times, and may have been somewhat effective, but it was unable to stop the rampant explosion of abnormal cell growth. So much has been learned about the different types of cancer in the last 40 years that we are not even sure what kind of cancer our mother actually had. Like so many trials and errors of that time, no one is sure if the information given us, or the treatment given her, was accurate by today's standards. But at the time, it was the best they knew to do.

Over the next several months, Mama spent a great deal of time in Huntsville with Martha and George, partly because her doctors were there, and partly because Martha did not want her mother to be alone when she was ill. Sometime during that period, Tullahoma opened a brand new nursing home that was affiliated with the Harton Hospital. The girls made several trips there to check to see if the nursing and the care would provide a suitable place for Mama. Finally, they decided to take her for a personal tour to see what she thought of the place. Mama decided that there were a lot of old people out there, and she wanted no part of it. It certainly wasn't like staying in Huntsville, and being waited on by Martha. Finally they introduced her to a couple of ladies, and she found she had a friend there and her attitude softened. She found out that it wasn't all that bad having meals prepared for her every day, a brand new room t stay in, and a full time nurse to tend to her. She settled in after that and made several new friends. It was a good solution for everybody, especially with the full resources of the hospital available to her, and the frequent visits from children and grandchildren. Mama had a parade of people visiting her, while some rarely had a visitor. The fact that many of the residents were somewhat jealous of all the attention this "new girl" was getting may have even been a source of pride for her. She loved to introduce her children around to the other residents, and they must have wondered, *"How many children does this woman have?"*

The Proper Thing

The hour of departure has arrived and we go our ways; I to die, and you to live.
Which is better? Only God knows.
        Socrates

Mama died on March 31, 1971, the victim of having 10 children pass through her frail body. No records exist for miscarriages, although relatives claim she had more than one.

She never lived to enjoy any of the major successes of the nine children that she single- handedly raised, which took nearly every waking moment of her adult life. She died too young for that, at age 64, but I think she did realize, and take pride in the fact that, as one-by- one we all "graduated" from under her roof, that each of us was capable of being independent and self-reliant. She also knew that we were all mentally and physically tough enough to take advantage of opportunities. We'd been tested, and we had all passed. She was well aware of all our individual strengths and weaknesses.

When the last of her nine children had finished college, she quietly passed away after her three year battle with the most dreaded disease of our time. It had finally spread to organs necessary for survival. All of us had rallied to be with her on those final days. The official cause of her death was kidney failure. It only takes a couple of weeks when the renal system shuts down, and it was a medically predictable result. Everyone knew it was coming. With Horace, Martha, Tommy and Sara standing by her bed, she took her final breath.

In all our years under her watch, she held steadfast to an unspoken rule, that the oldest child, that is, the next to leave the nest, was entitled to the lion's share of available resources. The rest of us would just have to sacrifice until it was our time. She was consistent with this rule. Then when the last one found her wings and took a job in Atlanta, Mama just let go of the rope. The resources were gone. Her job was done. She gave up the ghost. Her life as a mother was over.

At her funeral service, the new Methodist preacher was extremely complimentary of our mother; the woman who insisted that we all go to church, but rarely got to attend church herself. She was too busy ironing shirts and spanking us out the door. Besides, she was tired, and needed some time to herself. She would listen to the Sunday service on the radio, sing along with the hymns, and get some needed rest. It was our turn to memorize the Ten Commandments. She knew what they were.

We all began as Methodists, but it didn't matter to her where we went to church, as long as we went. When we were old enough to make up our own minds, we usually went where our friends went, especially if it meant holding hands with them. But at that moment, we all happened to be in the same pew at the same time at The United Methodist Church in Tullahoma, Tennessee at the funeral service of Margaret Dryden Willis.

Over the years, preachers had come and gone in that little church, and Mother had known every one of them. Ironically, the one that was preaching her funeral service had been there only a few months, and he knew less about her and her children than any of them. In fact, I can say with complete certainty, that he was absolutely clueless. The main theme of his eulogy seemed to focus on Mother's penchant, according to him, of doing "the proper thing." Apparently, in interactions with her, he remembered that she had requested his assistance in some matter, and asked him to advise her on the proper thing to do. He focused his remarks that day on those three words.

So this is how we were all to remember her, I guess, as someone who insisted on doing the proper thing. But he had only written some church-speak for a person he couldn't even begin to understand. We knew that he knew nothing about this saintly woman lying there in front of him in that box. In contrast, we also knew that she knew everything that was going on. She was observing every one of us, just like she always did. All nine of her grown ducklings were sitting there in two neat little rows, in our Sunday best, having to know that Mama was looking in on all of this, and judging it all from every possible perspective, all at the same time. She knew what every single one of her children was wearing, and what each of us was thinking. And we all knew she knew. She knew just about everything, because she had lived through just about everything in the last 64 years. Anything she didn't know, she didn't need to know. She was a magnificent woman, and the man preaching her service may as well have been the man who read our water meter.

She also knew that, even though she had been sick for a long time, and was worn out from it, her funeral was happening much too soon, and if she had her way it would have been this way or that. But it was too late for all that. She couldn't control everything. Not now anyway. So we all had to sit there, and swallow his words, while we watched her slip out of our lives, comforted somewhat by knowing that she had suffered long enough; "*a gracious plenty*," as she would have put it. We were saying goodbye to our beloved mother. Dear, sweet Margaret, revered by all who knew her, having a proper funeral.

She left precious little in the way of an estate. Except for a few trinkets and a lot of good memories, we were it. Her children were her legacy.

After the service, her sons and sons-in-law would serve as pall bearers while we executed Mama's unwritten will. She had only asked for two things. She asked that her favorite hymn be sung, and that she would be taken to Moore's Chapel Cemetery in Bluestocking Hollow, to be buried close to her mom and dad. Ashes to ashes, she would complete the circle and go home. We loaded her and her modest casket into the late model black hearse provided by Dave Culbertson's Funeral Home, and began the somber procession through the little town that raised us. To our astonishment, people were standing along the streets quietly watching the hearse-led caravan slowly pass, as though someone famous was going away. Not a huge crowd, just here and there a few people standing along the road in front of their stores and homes for the several miles it took to drive through Tullahoma. It gave me a 10 minute chill bump. At the city limits, we broke the bonds of that little town, and I realized that Mama was going home. No tears would come, only stunned silence.

It was a cold and blustery day, but the sun was bright, just like I imagined many of her days in her one room school house. Even though it was the first of April, there was a frozen base of patchy snow on the ground at Bluestocking, just like the night that Pete left home 24 years ago, almost to the day. I knew that she hated the cold but she didn't complain. She accepted it gracefully. The same way she girded herself for every other wish that didn't come true. She made the best of it. After all, spring would be just around the corner.

The preacher said a few more eloquent, generic phrases, and we lowered her into the frozen ground. A few minutes later, we shook his hand and mumbled our thanks from the family. We had prepared an envelope for him, as was the custom. The proper thing, you know. Then we loaded our own lifeless bodies into the waiting vehicles, some of the engines left running to keep warm. We were just going to leave her there, I guess. As all the cars were winding down the little gravel path that served as a road, I turned to have one last look at her peaceful resting place. Her favorite hymn played inside my head.

"On a hill, far away, stood an old rugged cross
An emblem of suffering and shame"

I spent the better part of two days with my mother a couple of days before she passed away, but was not by her side when she died. I remember how awkward and immature I felt trying to comfort her. She just looked at me as if to say, *"It's ok."* She wanted me to rub her back. It comforted her. I lay on top of the sheets beside her, and put my arm around her and she held my hand. She didn't want to go to sleep. Several people I had never seen before came by to visit, and told me nice things about her. They kept interrupting my time with her. She knew what was happening, and I knew she was afraid, but I didn't know what to do. I had seen a lot of good people die, and there were many times when I thought I would be one of them. But we only get to have one mother.

Now, I know exactly what I should have done, and what I should have said. I should have thanked her. I didn't get to do that. I was too overwhelmed. I read somewhere that if the only prayer you ever said was *"thank you,"* that would suffice. I should have looked into her eyes, and said, *"Thank you, Mama, for all you did for me."* Perhaps, if I had done that, she would not have been afraid. I picture her smiling up at me, and squeezing my hand when I tell her this. But it did not get said. I hope she will forgive me.

I have written this book for her to tell her what I failed to tell her then.

Thank you, Mama.

HORACE

Horace and Marie had one daughter, Alicia Lynn Willis, born on 29 November, 1954. He eventually received his high school equivalent diploma through night school and correspondence. His wife, Marie, died at age 50, on March 24, 1981, of a cancer-related illness. Horace experienced a heart attack when he was 50 and had open heart by-pass surgery. In 1983 he married Rebecca Long. Two years later, at age 55, he had a fatal heart attack while jogging alone after work on Halloween evening, October 31, 1985. Ironically, this was Marie's birth date. Rebecca honored the family's wish to bury him beside his deceased wife's body at Rose Hill Cemetery near Tullahoma. He was survived by his daughter, Alicia, his adopted stepson, Jimmy Lance, and two grandsons, Hunter and Cameron Myatt. (Alicia and Ronnie Myatt)

Horace, age 14

MARTHA

Martha Willis and George Thrower still live in Huntsville, Alabama. She left work in June of 1961, after 10 years, to start a family. George Robert Thrower, Jr. was born on September, 26, 1962. George, Sr. retired in 2000. They spend time in Florida and enjoy travel.

Martha, age 17

ANN

Ann and Buddy Martin are both retired and live in Donelson, Tennessee, just outside Nashville. She worked for Scott Clayton Insurance Company for 22 years. In 1997, at age 62, she achieved her lifelong goal of attaining her college degree from David Lipscomb University. They have two sons, David and Steven, and 4 grandchildren, Ryan and Marty (David and Denice) and Eric and Dillon (Steve and Laura).

Ann, age 17

TOMMY

Tommy worked as an electrical engineer with AEDC until 1981. In 1985 he discovered the ministry, and became an ordained minister. He was attending Dallas Theological Center, in Dallas Texas when he was diagnosed with lung cancer during a routine physical examination. Three weeks later, on November 17, 1997 at age 61, he died at Baylor Medical Center in Dallas while undergoing a normal chemotherapy treatment. He was buried at Rose Hill Cemetery near his brother Horace.

Tommy, age 19

SARA

Sara and David Reichnau live in Tullahoma, Tennessee and have two sons, David Keith born on April 7, 1969 and Benton Douglas, born July 25, 1970. Sara retired from nursing in 1995. Her husband retired as an aeronautical engineer at AEDC in 2000. They enjoy spending time with their grandchildren, Lincoln (Ben and Kendra) and Payton (David and Beth).

Sara, age 18

BUDDY

Bud is retired after 34 years in the securities business as a partner with J.C. Bradford and Company, and now lives in Naples, Florida. In 1963, he married Kay Fleming Willis of Columbus, Mississippi, and they raised two sons, Kirk McGuire Willis, Born February 7, 1966, and Kevin Dryden Willis, born March 26, 1969. Bud is now married to Susan Lee Barnes. In 1975, he was named Tennessee's Outstanding Young Man. In Pensacola he served as the Commissioning Chairman of the USS Mitscher, a Naval Destroyer commissioned in December 1994. He has one granddaughter, Rachel (Kirk and Elva).

Buddy, age 21

TYKIE

Tykie graduated from Middle Tennessee State University in 1968, and worked in the hospitality industry for Mark Inn in Atlanta, and as a public relations representative for Holiday Inn in Nashville. On Saturday, July 28, 1974, at age 30, while traveling alone to visit his brother Tommy, he was involved in a head-on collision in Manchester, Tennessee. The accident took his life as well as the lives of two people in the other vehicle. He was the first sibling to be buried at Rose Hill Cemetery, and would later be joined by his two brothers, Horace (1985), and Tommy (1997). It is an odd coincidence that the oldest child of each of the three sets of nine children are now deceased, and buried within a few feet of each other at Rose Hill Cemetary.

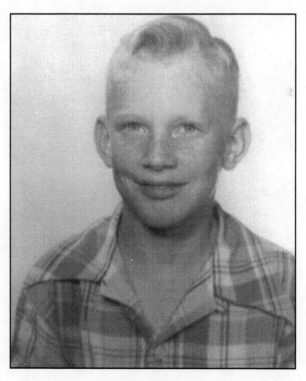

Tykie, age 12

BEAU

Beau graduated from Middle Tennessee State University in Murfreesboro, Tennessee, and served a tour of duty in the U.S. Army. He was stationed in Germany, making and fitting eyewear for his fellow soldiers. He was married to Jan Blair of Tullahoma for ten years. He has remained loyal to the eyewear industry, first working for Bausch and Lomb, and owning his own optical shop in Memphis for 20 years. He now lives in Olive Branch, Mississippi, and works for the Southern College of Optometry in Memhis.

Beau, age 3

LINDA

Linda graduated from the University of Memphis in 1969, and has taught French for 35 years in the Coffee County School System. She studied acting and dance at Herbert Berghof Studio in New York. She travels frequently, and periodically teaches during the summer in Paris, France.

Linda with Mama, age 8 and 6

BURR (PETE) WILLIS

We had no contact with our father from the day he left in 1947. He died 30 years later of a cancer-related illness in Atlanta, Georgia. We were notified of his death by one of his friends, who asked if we would bear the expense of his burial. His funeral was unattended by any of his children.

(Riding off in the sunset?)

Epilogue

Historical Outtakes

It is historically significant to our family that Bedford County and Shelbyville were founded and chartered in 1807 by one of the elder Thomas Dryden's relatives by marriage, Daniel McKissick, a commissioner. When Tennessee originally founded the county, it encompassed 2000 square miles, and included all of Lincoln and Moore counties as well as part of Marshall and Coffee counties. All this was a "gift" from the Indians because the Treaties of Tellico and Dearborn destroyed all the rights of the Indians to any part of the land that is now Middle Tennessee. The signing of these treaties caused a rush of homesteaders to pour across the divide between the Stones River and the Duck River.

The Duck River runs through the middle of the county, and was a main attraction for the settlers. Transportation would have been difficult to say the least, but trails left by wild animals and Indians were soon widened to accommodate carts and wagons. Travel required imagination and determination, and one of the most difficult challenges was fording the Duck River. Finally, the first river bridge was built in 1832, and what is believed to be one of the first turnpikes was built in 1834, running from Shelbyville to Murfreesboro and eventually to Nashville.

Even before there were roads, before there were schools, merchants, banks, or railroads, there were religious gatherings. Church is where you went to christen a child, marry a son or daughter, and bury friends and neighbors. The center of community life was the church.

It was home. The high point of the year in early Bedford County was Muster Day. Held in accordance with Congressional militia laws, this was the day that every man in the county subject to military service reported to the county seat to drill, "armed and equipped as the law directs." Although they filled the requirements of the law, they did not miss the opportunity to turn Muster Day into a celebration. There were shooting matches, wrestling contests, tales to be told, and political speeches to be made. This may have been where many young couples were introduced to each other.

The county got its name from one of the more rugged personalities of that area, Nathan Bedford Forrest (1821-1877) of Chapel Hill, Tennessee. Forrest was the "John Wayne" of his time and made his reputation during the Civil War promoting the advantages of horses. Before Forrest was a twinkle in his mother's eye, William Dryden (1795-1877) and Thomas Dryden (1796-1863), both sons of Jonathan Dryden, came to Tennessee in about 1810. In 1814 William served for several months as a sergeant in the Tennessee Militia under General Andrew Jackson. Apparently, he encountered some difficulty in collecting his pay for these services, and on Dec. 1, 1815, he had to sue for the money due him. Later, he obtained a Federal Pension as a result of his war services. He married Abigail Colwell Henderson and they had 11 children. In 1829, he walked 400 miles to Illinois to look at some land and walked back to Bedford County. He packed up his family and moved them there. He was the great grandfather of Robert L. (Bob) Young, who came to Tullahoma in 1956 to head the University of Tennessee Space Institute. In all the years that the Young family and the Willis family lived in Tullahoma, none of us knew that we were related until the writing of this book.

William's brother, Thomas (1876-1863), established a home on a farm in Bedford County in Bluestocking Hollow, about 12 miles from Shelbyville, in 1824. Thomas also served in the War of 1812 in Porter's and Dickinson's Tennessee Militia. Thomas married Mary Henderson Dickson (1806-1878), and had three sons. The first born was Nathaniel Lewis Dryden (1839-1916), who had 10 children with Sarah Jane Lewellyn (1844-1916). One of those ten, Thomas Floyd Dryden (1883-1937), was my grandfather.

Thomas' older sister, Margaret, married Horace White who had a sister named Emma Mae White. The White family was a well regarded family in Bluestocking. Margaret's marriage to Mr. White turned out to be very convenient for Thomas, because he courted and married his new brother-in-law's sister, Emma Mae, and they produced five children, the oldest being Margaret Louise Dryden, my mother. To say that all these people had a predisposition to hardship is an understatement in today's terms, but apparently the rugged life they "enjoyed" was a routine matter then, because those early years would turn out to be some of the fondest memories of my mother's life.

Emma Mae would come to be known to us as Granny, the quint-essential grandmother, right out of a Norman Rockwell painting. She is shown milking a cow in front of this book with my two oldest sisters. Thomas Floyd Dryden (1883-1937) and Emma Mae (White) Dryden (1885-1971) still reside together in Bluestocking Hollow. They lie side by side in two small grave plots and share the same headstone at Moore's Chapel Cemetery. This place was home to them and where they had raised my mother and their four other children. The term 'bluestocking' originally referred to privileged ladies, seeking a more sophisticated, literate lifestyle. Ironically, this place is out in the sticks about 12 miles from nowhere. More suitable to blue overalls than blue stockings, in its early years only the most rugged pioneers would have dared to tackle that territory. In fact, in the early 1800's, the whole of Bedford County was nothing but dense canebrakes and vast forests. To most people it would have been considered impenetrable.

Floyd Emma's young family survived the rigors of WW I (1913-1918) in typical farm fashion, with the usual early morning milking and plenty of butter and eggs. Mama had a younger sister, Virginia (1910-1978), and three younger brothers, James Howard (1914-1982), Floyd (1917-1997), and Lewis Gordon (1920-1984). Her three brothers grew up to be typical farm boys who could do almost anything, and everyone pitched in to help keep the place operating smoothly. They were ideal brothers, hard working and happy. Mama's little sister, 4 years younger, seemed to receive a little more coddling than the others and all this made for a typical American family, full of love and personal attention.

My grandfather, Thomas Dryden, lived a good life for 54 years and took an afternoon nap almost every day of his adult life. I hesitate to say that he died suddenly because everybody does. Rather, he died unexpectedly of sudden heart failure on 14 July 1937. His sons were 23, 20 and 17 at the time of his death. He had a short history of symptoms that were interpreted in those days as "heart problems." This unfortunate bit of family history became an unavoidable genetic trait for many of his progeny, including this writer, who has four stents in his coronary arteries.

The Great Depression (1929-1933) had extracted its pound of flesh on the banking system and economies of that area. Anyone owing money on any asset was extremely challenged. The burden of keeping up the family farm in Bluestocking was too great. There was an interim period where the family did some sharecropping on another small farm, but as soon as the U.S. entered World War II, all three of the boys were called into service, and sharecropping was no longer a viable option because the boys did most of the work. Farming was, and still is, a family affair. Virginia was the only child left at home with Granny. Margaret was married and already had six children by the time the U.S. entered the War. Granny and her schoolteacher daughter Virginia found a small, more manageable house closer to town (Shelbyville), and moved in together.

My grandfather Thomas's obituary described him as a very popular citizen, who made friends easily. He got along well with people, including his only son in law (my father). They liked and respected each other, although I am certain that my mother and father had many financial issues of their own that did not contribute positively to the overall family finances. Virginia (Turner) was 27 when her father died, and she never took a husband. Including this writer, my mother gave Emma Mae nine grandchildren. Her brother Lewis Gordon ("L.G.") was the only one of her children to give her another grandchild, Sherry Lynn (1953).

Granny Dryden was a 95 pound, wiry little, white-haired Christmas pixie. She always smelled like the frosting on a fresh baked coconut cake, and her refrigerator smelled like vanilla ice cream. I can't imagine that she ever spanked a child. She probably didn't need to, because it was impossible to misbehave around her. After her husband died, she managed another 35 years as a single woman. The extent to which she remained determined and independent throughout her life is best illustrated by the story of her annual jam cake ritual.

Every year around Thanksgiving, Granny made her special jam cake for the holidays. She then put the cake in the attic so it would stay safe and cool while the ingredients got better acquainted. She was a short lady, only five feet tall, and could not reach the rope to pull down the attic steps, so she always used a three legged milking stool to stand on. This aggravated all three of her sons who thought using that stool was far too dangerous for her, especially while trying to juggle a heavy cake. They tried everything to discourage these antics; including cutting the rope so short that even with the stool she couldn't reach it. Somehow, the jam cake always found its way into the attic, even after they severed the rope completely. No one knew how she did it, but no one was going to tell the Christmas pixie where she could or could not put her Christmas cake.

The War (1941-1945) was a grueling time for Granny, with her three sons gone, and it caused her to age dramatically in appearance. Oddly, she seemed to age all at once, and then stayed the same little, gray headed grandmother for as long as we knew her. She worried constantly about her boys during the War. She covered this with her strong faith and her pleasant nature. Whenever she worried, she would sing or hum one her favorite hymns. And she hummed many hymns during that War. But hardship to her was like pouring water on a duck. She could handle it. Her boys served admirably, and all came home safely, but not totally unscathed. James Howard (Howard) was awarded the Silver Star for gallantry during a battle in France when he assumed command of his unit after its commander was wounded, and led an attack that destroyed four enemy machine gun positions. He also received the Purple Heart from injuries received when he was buried alive by a bomb blast, and had to dig his way out. The three men loved their mother dearly, wrote often, and were very attentive to their widowed mother throughout her life.

All five of Emma's children attended and graduated from that one room school near Bluestocking. That building is gone now, along with the Dryden home place. The little church is gone too, but the cemetery is still there, cared for and well maintained by Brent

Davidson. The Davidson family also dates back to the beginnings of Bluestocking.

Many of the White family are buried there, including Horace White, Granny's brother.

After her three sons all made it home from the War, "*in one piece,*" they sought various jobs near home. Howard and Floyd opened a grocery store, which they called Dryden's Grocery and operated it for several years. Later Howard did some farming and spent a considerable amount of time as a butcher in the grocery business. Floyd was a skilled appliance repairman and eventually opened a retail appliance store in Shelbyville that seemed to be very successful. L.G., or "Legs" as we referred to him, the youngest of the three boys, worked at the Empire Pencil Company for several years and eventually went to work as an engraver for Jostens, a company that produces high school yearbooks, class rings and school memorabilia. Virginia taught elementary school most of her adult life and became one of the most well known teachers in Shelbyville, having taught hundreds of kids to read and write during her 45 year career as a first grade teacher. She never tired of teaching kids to read, and kept a large collection of children's books in her home, which she offered freely to her young visitors.

Much of the Dryden family history was provided by Sherry Lynn Dryden Sorrells, of Lewisburg, Tennessee, the Daughter of L.G. Dryden, one of mama's three brothers.

THE WILLIS FAMILY

There are many distinguished men with the name of Willis in England and this family descended from William Willis who eventually settled in Virginia. His only known son was Thomas Willis who died in Marshall County, TN in March of 1845. Thomas's son Davis Willis was actually the first to move to Tennessee, but his father soon followed him to Marshall County. Davis and Martha (Hughes) Willis had five children, one of whom was my great-grandfather, Thomas Hughes Willis, born on December 26, 1835. Thomas had six children, the oldest of which was Alby Leon Willis, born on 16 Feb., 1861. Alby was a farmer and mule trader. Alby's nickname was John and he had 10 children with Cynthia Pinkney Glenn. My father was the youngest of the six boys.

One of Alby's peers and good friends at the time was Lem Motlow of neighboring Lynchburg, Tennessee, the manager of Jack Daniels Distillery. Most of the whiskey that was made by Jack Daniels at that time was sold by the barrel. Alby, being in the mule business, hauled empty barrels for Motlow and had access to the basement under which the full barrels of whiskey were stored. Alby drilled a hole through the boards in the ceiling, and was able to penetrate one of the barrels to siphon off a steady supply for his own personal use. So this is part of the Willis legacy, I guess, that my grandfather stole whiskey from Jack Daniels. Alby eventually moved to Altus, Oklahoma and lived there with his wife until he died on 23 November, 1941. I was born about 3 months later on 2 September, 1941, five days before the Japanese bombed Pearl Harbor.

Alby had another son, whom he named after himself and also nicknamed John. The younger Alby suffered fits of depression and mental stress, and he often left home for months at a time without anyone knowing where he was, or when he might return. One of his sons was named David, who currently lives near Tampa Florida with his wife Peggy. They are the only Willises that remain in contact with Margaret's children. David's younger brother, John Harlan, is mentioned in this book as having been awarded the Congressional Medal of Honor, one of eight Tennesseans so honored in WWII.

Acknowlegements

There are people that do things for us every day, and rarely get thanked. This page is dedicated to them.

I appreciate generosity more than any other human trait. It took me a long time to realize that gratefulness and generosity are close cousins, and the keys to a happy life. And that selfishness is the ultimate form of immaturity. My business career was a lot more fun, and life in general was more enjoyable after I began to practice what I had learned. My schoolteacher aunt tried to tell me that it's not how you give a gift but how you receive one that shows the kind of person you really are. I had to grow up to know what she meant. Our true character lies in the way we express our thanks. The following people have been very generous with their time and resources in helping me in various ways in the writing of this book.

Carl Andrews at OfficeMax Impress, printing, organization and proof reading

Janice Antel, typing and computer skills

Gary Draper, proofreading and editing

Sherry Sorrells, Dryden genealogy

Mike Steinberg, advice

The Tullahoma News and Larry Nee, research

David and Peggy Willis, genealogy

Lee Willis, best friend and supporter

Chuck Ardezzone, CEO, IntroubleZone, cover design

All my siblings, for supplying the stories.

Tullahoma High School Class of 1959 Fifty Year Reunion Speech

By Bud Willis...Jun 6, 2009
Introduced by Ray Bailey

There goes K. Ray Bailey, the guy who stole all the popsicles out of the cafeteria after basketball practice, and then went on to become a college president. I'll bet you didn't put that on your resume did you Mr. Big.

Well...this is scary! But I feel eerily calm...like you do just before you have a seizure.

Some of you are looking at me like you don't know who I am. We had lunch together, remember?

It feels good to be back among friends.

As I looked down the list of names of our graduating class, I couldn't help but notice something. We all got along with each other. I can't remember ever not getting along with a single one of you. That's impressive!

Especially considering that I haven't gotten along with anybody since.

I confess that I never really made a lot of friends after high school. I know this because, I keep getting these gushy emails from people who want me to forward it to 15 friends, and I will receive a miracle.

First of all, I don't have 15 friends.

I don't even know 15 people that I can tolerate.

Mostly, because of those stupid emails!

At any rate, I'm getting screwed out of a lot of miracles.

I need some luck right now. I'm supposed to entertain you people and you're not even drinking. I must have been, when I agreed to do this.

You should know; it wasn't easy to get someone to speak to you.

They first asked the funniest person in our class and were turned down.

Then they went after the best looking person in the class and were refused again.

Finally, they asked the most humble.

And I just couldn't say no...three times in a row.

I used that same joke 30 years ago.

I knew you wouldn't remember it.

Not knowing what kind of mood you might be in, I wrote two different monologues.

One is a motivational challenge to inspire us to be better people, and to make a difference in the world.

The other is mostly foolishness and humorous nonsense.

So, what'll it be....decaf or regular?

It's good to see you haven't changed!

I only had one speech anyway.

The best speech is one that has a good beginning and a good ending, and the two should be as close together as possible.

Most of you have probably already gotten what you came here for, having a good time catching up!

So why do we even need a speaker?

Well, for one thing this is a milestone.

We're lucky to be here.

Especially you, Colyar!

We have survived a lot of crazy things in 67 years.

If nothing else, we need to pay tribute to that.

Our graduation was a half century ago.

So, while I won't take long up here, I'm also not going to rush this.

So just pop another Prozac.

The best way to get through this is to relax and lower your expectations.

Set your snooze alarm for 15 minutes.

Just long enough for me to peek under your hood, and see if there might be a teenage motor still purring under there.

Speaking of teenagers, I don't see DON CORNELIUS on the list tonight.

He has changed less than any of us.

Last we heard, he was living on a houseboat.

Why he would want to live on a houseboat, parked in his front yard, we have no idea.

So, this is the way it's supposed to work, my job is to say funny things and your job is to laugh. But if you get finished with your job before I do, don't leave me hanging up here.

This is our Golden Anniversary!

If you don't remember what gold is, it's that stuff we used to have before our stock brokers took it somewhere and had it bronzed.

The last few years have been a wild ride for retirees.

They've thrown global warming, global terrorism and a global financial meltdown at us, and we're still standing.

For eight years we had a President that wouldn't speak to us… and now, we've got one that won't shut up.

It took us 30 years to get our houses paid for and now they're giving them away on the courthouse steps.

And it seems like every time we get a little money ahead, along comes another one of these expensive chicken dinners.

History has never seen anything like this.

In previous years, when we got a check returned from the bank that was stamped "insufficient funds"...

They weren't talking about the bank.

Fifty years ago there was a very funny joke going around about a Mexican who came to his first American ball game.

He was impressed that they sang to him before the game, "Jose, can you see?"

It's funny how that's not funny anymore.

Jose and all his buddies have a ringside seat now.

Whether we voted for change or not, we're getting it.

Someone suggested that if we lined up all the politicians in the country end to end....that would probably be... a good idea.

But as you remember from our senior trip there, Washington, DC makes people do strange things.

So, the theme of my little talk is, "We made it."

I thought about giving a talk on memory loss, but I couldn't think of anything.

Looking out at all of you, I can see that we all have plenty to be thankful for, but right now, at the top of my list, is <u>Name Tags!</u>

Whoever invented 'em, God bless 'em.

We all prepared ourselves for this reunion the same way, by thumbing through the yearbook so we would recognize everyone.

In retrospect, how stupid was that!

There is no possible way to prepare for this.

Ironically, in the short time we've been together today it's obvious that we have more in common now than we did then.

Medicare, Social Security, AARP and ARTHRITIS, to name a few!

Not to mention the pharmaceuticals that got us here.

Forget Viagra…it comes with a blood pressure warning so we can't touch that.

It must be for much younger people.

Now, they tell us they have a pill from a red wine derivative that can add 20 years to our lives.

Well, that's a hoot.

We've been going straight for the bottle!

We might have had that pill a little sooner if David Spradling hadn't totaled our science lab.

But, I'm not going to stand up here for 10 minutes and drone on about the aging process.

I have far too much respect for old people than that.

The point is "we made it."

Psychologists don't know why people travel thousands of miles to attend these high school reunions.

Some believe the #1 reason that men come back is to see old girlfriends.

I can buy into that theory. Men are real stupid that way.

I'm looking at some right now.

But you can't blame them.

We had a bunch of good looking girls in our class.

I'm looking at some right now.

And ladies, if I may, I think I can speak for all the guys when I say to you…that, seeing you again like this… after all these years… it's enough to bring tears to our eyes.

But on the other side of that coin, any woman who came here to reconnect with an old boyfriend, needs to take a quick look around the room.

Then go home and take a long, hard look at your life.

And I would hope that you would schedule an appointment with your therapist, first thing Monday morning.

Let's face it, there isn't enough testosterone left in this room to stir a glass of Metamucil.

Fellas, we are facing the unthinkable.

Yes, the good news is, we made it here, but the bad news could be our worst fear…we may outlive our genitals.

I don't care who you are, that's funny.

You weren't ready for that one.

Humor is not always pretty.

If you don't get back to your home town very often, one of the first things that you might think of doing is to drive around town to see what's changed.

Try to get some old memories flowing.

Is the house that you grew up in still standing?

Some of them have been torn down. Not surprising!

Who would want to live in a house after we got through with it?

But worse than that, guess what! Moon's is gone!

What's up with that?

What was wrong with Moon's?

Did they have a grease fire?

The drive in movie is closed down, too.

Maybe we should have paid to get in… instead of hiding in the trunk of the car!

Maybe we should have been more sensitive to the owner's cash flow, his profit margins and overhead expenses...........NAAAH-HH!

Even the Marshall Theater is gone!

What the heck are kids supposed to do anymore?

NO WONDER PEOPLE ARE MOVING TO ESTILL SPRINGS.

I think we have had maybe 5 or 6 of these reunions since 1959.

Remember the first one when we actually tried to lose a few pounds?

That didn't work!

For the second one I quit drinking.

That really didn't work!

One time, I even brought a nice girlfriend with me, and introduced her around to some of you.

I MISS HER!

Never saw her again.

The last one I came to, I drank too much, and don't remember very much about it.

So, I guess that one was my favorite!

But, you know what!

I think we have never looked better, and you have to love the energy in this room.

We can do a lot of things now that we couldn't back then.

At our age, we can hide our own Easter eggs.

We can make the same noises as our coffee maker.

Our imaginations are more active than ever, and we have more time to read.

What man in this room doesn't enjoy curling up with a good book...like the Victoria's Secret catalog?

And best of all! We can still drive at night.

Scares the hell out of people, but we still do it.

We drove here, and we made it!

The real reason we come back to these reunions is to recapture some of those childhood feelings and memories.

Those were the most carefree times of our lives, and can never be replaced.

The pimples, the proms, the chigger bites and all.

A chance to put the blue jeans back on for a little while!

How exciting it was to get our drivers license!

Working on the homecoming parade float!

There wasn't a roll of toilet paper in school after that.

The memories start out as a trickle and become a flood.

If we're lucky, the endorphins kick in a little bit.

Let's face it, we all influenced and changed each other in some way.

We come back, to reconnect with the people who shaped us into who we are today.

I'd like to think that there might be one or two of you that are a little bit funnier because of me.

(Or maybe you gave up humor altogether.)

Certainly we had good teachers, and they did teach us useful things, like good manners and the four basic food groups.

But none of that compares to the influence of our friends when we're growing up.

Our teachers didn't show us how to drive a car.

SW Stone showed me.

And I showed him... how to get it out of a ditch.

So we helped each other.

Coming to a class reunion is just another way of saying THANK YOU for what we all meant to each other.

So, maybe, that's why we pack our bags and travel hundreds of miles to these things. (Sniff!)

And…what the hell …we get to see old girlfriends!

We also come to remember that we grew up in a simpler time.

Values were different then.

We didn't do drugs!!!!!

We do them now….but…this is getting confusing.

I did a lot of research for a book I wrote about growing up in Tullahoma.

And I learned that our generation had to endure a strange period of post war paranoia.

TV may have depicted the Fifties as the "Happy Days" but in reality our parents and teachers were driving us nuts with scary tales of polio, radiation induced cancer, nuclear attacks, and crispy kids burning up in school buildings.

We practiced atomic bomb drills at school.

Remember those things? We were instructed to duck down and put our heads under our desks.

Now, I was not a bright student.

But somehow, I think we all knew, that little desk was highly overrated.

Our parents made us buy shoes that didn't fit, so we would "grow into them."

At the shoe store, they had us stick our feet in radioactive machines just to see our toes wiggle.

These were the people who were supposed to protect us.

No wonder we peed in the bed.

We practiced football in 90 degree heat and the coaches wouldn't let us have water…and there were no faceguards on our helmets.

What were they thinking?

Our parents were more obsessing over whether our underwear was clean enough to be in a car wreck.

It's a wonder we had clean underwear.

It was a perfect storm for confused teenagers.

Ozzie and Harriet may have seemed normal enough on TV but look how trashy little Ricky turned out.

We survived Lucky Strikes and Philip Morris.

We were told that fine tobacco is its own best filter, and that "Pall Mall, famous cigarettes, are outstanding! And they are mild.

You can light either end."

(Just not in the school rest room)

From all this chaos, our own American idols were dropping like flies.

Bobby Daren, the Big Bopper, Buddy Holly, James Dean, Marilyn Monroe, Natalie Wood, Hank Williams, and my own personal favorite.

Elvis Presley!

Thank you very much.

Earlier I told you that I thumbed through my yearbook.

I was just kidding about that.

I couldn't find mine either.

But I do remember the names of the two people that were voted most likely to succeed.

One of them was Mary Ann Jackson who hasn't attended a single one of these things.

In fifty years, we haven't succeeded in finding her.

We tried Google, People Pages and My Space with no luck.

We should have named her most likely to disappear without a trace.

We did find her male counterpart, Austin Carr, just outside Nashville practicing radiology.

He is here tonight. And I have great news.

He has offered to donate 100,000 dollars to our slush fund for future parties.

I made that up, but that's what I'd do if I was a rich doctor.

So what is success anyway?

We don't have the 100 grand and we can't find Mary Ann.

Who came up with the ridiculous notion of class superlatives?

We were all superlative. This had to be another bad idea trumped up by the faculty to keep us all in line.

I personally believe that it was all based on what you wrote in the yearbook under your picture; like that was supposed to define us for life or something.

Anyway, Austin took it pretty seriously and came up with this little beauty.

Here's his quote: "Explore the thought. Examine the asking eye."

What the heck is that supposed to mean?

We thought you wanted to be an optometrist.

I think that anyone in this room would have to say, that is a little over the top for a 17 year old.

But the faculty must have liked it.

And he was named "most likely to succeed."

Let's compare that to what my poker playing buddy James Boatman said. Boatman wrote.

And I know his wife Jane must have been proud of him when she read this.

Do only what you can't get out of doing."

Boatman was not named "most likely to succeed."

But if you examine that quote carefully, it is the epitome of good leadership and the art of delegation.

He may have been ahead of his time then, and misunderstood, BUT, if he can remain true to this core belief, and we ever have a 100 year reunion, he gets my vote as the most likely to be there for it.

So, have we really learned anything after high school?

Yes we have…we've learned how to beat the odds in a tough world.

And a lot of things they never taught us in a classroom.

We've learned, for example, to never go to a doctor that has recently purchased a big boat.

Unless you want to make his payments!

We've learned that we'd sooner be dead than to try to drink the recommended eight glasses of water every day.

We've learned that the only thing that eating a big breakfast does for us is make us want to eat a big lunch and a big dinner.

And we've also learned that most of the things that happen in life are not the result of careful planning.

It's more like John Lennon said, "Life is what happens when you are busy making other plans."

While everybody seems to be trying to accomplish something big, we seem to forget that life is really made up of a lot of little things, that need to get done every day.

So, here's the climax. (REMEMBER THOSE THINGS?)

If we could count all the people whose lives have been changed for the better because of the people in this room, and if we knew how many unemployed people had jobs because of us, (our own out-of-work children excepted, of course); if we could calculate our contribution to the gross domestic product; all the money we've raised and donated to charities; the people whose lives we've turned around; how many lives we've actually saved; all the communities we've served; if we knew all this, and how our children and grandchildren will continue doing these things, then we would have a more genuine perspective on the very superlative Tullahoma High School, Class of 1959.

Boys and girls, we are the living proof. We not only made it.

We made it a heck of a lot better than we found it.

And I leave here secure in the knowledge that not a single one of you would ever go around telling little kids that cigarette tobacco filters itself, nor would we ever make them stick their little feet into dangerous, radioactive machines, just so they can watch their toe bones wiggle.

Thank you….thank you very much!